CELEBRATING GOD'S WORLD IN CHILDREN'S CHURCH

A YEAR'S WORTH OF PRESCHOOL PROGRAMS

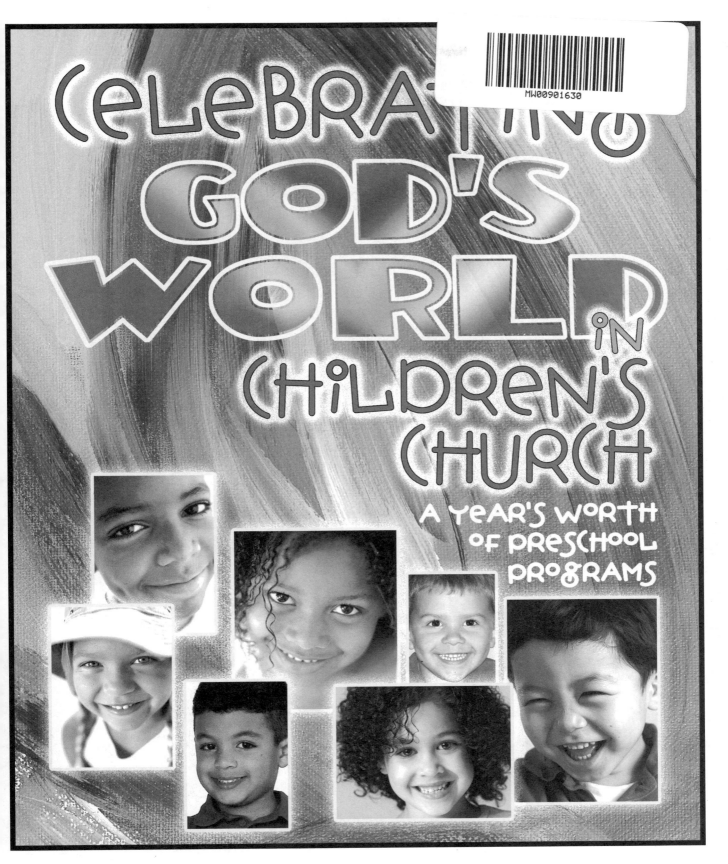

Abingdon Press

Nashville

Celebrating God's World in Children's Church

ISBN 0-687-05568-7

05 06 07 08 09 10 11 12 13 14—10 9 8 7 6 5 4 3 2 1

Dedicated to Gayle Taitt and Sue Cunningham,
who love the kids at our church, big and small.

CONTENTS

INTRODUCTION

READY TO CELEBRATE?

The goodness and grandeur of God's world is ready for you and your children to explore and celebrate in each of these fifty-five fun, faith-building programs! Whether Children's Church is as short as thirty minutes or runs an hour or more, this book has just what you need to provide an upbeat and kid-friendly experience for the children of your church.

THE VERSE:

Like adult worship, Children's Church is grounded in Scriptures. Beloved Bible verses, passages, and stories are the foundation for these programs.

THE MESSAGE:

Each program is centered around a simple yet meaningful point relating to God's world, from the magnificence of God's creatures to loving one another, to the birth of Jesus, our Savior.

TWIRLING:

Each week, a child will take a turn at spinning a globe as everyone joins in a happy chant and then twirls around. This fun warm-up will help settle the children for the program. If you aren't able to locate a globe, a blue or green plastic ball will do the trick.

SHARING:

Children love to share their opinions and experiences! A sharing time before the story will cut back on interruptions and will help children to turn their attention toward the theme. It's best to go from child to child, encouraging each to share. This benefits those who are too shy to raise their hands.

LISTENING:

Children will listen and pay attention to these lively stories. Sometimes the story calls for simple props or a bit of costume. Children are often asked to participate through motions and vocal responses.

PRAYING:

Following the story, lead children in prayer. While some prayers are more traditional, others engage the children more actively.

EXPLORING:

Through crafts, drama, adventures, games, songs, guest speakers, and hunts, children will explore, experience, and celebrate God's world. The activities are creative but not difficult. Care has been taken to use inexpensive and commonly available supplies. Although you may want a helper, especially if you have a large group, most activities can be led by one person.

SNACKING:

Each week, a creative snack will add to the fun and reinforce the program's message and story. Check with parents concerning food allergies. You will need bowls, cups, plates, napkins, and utensils for serving some of the snacks, and your choice of beverages.

SINGING:

Children love to sing and don't mind if your voice isn't star quality.

Two songs have been chosen for each lesson. The first is from *Wee Sing Bible Songs* published by Price Stern Sloan and available at both bookstores and discount stores. The second is from *FaithSongs* published by Abingdon Press and available at most Christian bookstores. You can purchase CDs for each book to use as listening/teaching tools and as accompaniment.

Feel free to substitute any song that you are familiar with that helps to fit the theme of the program. Have children march, dance, play rhythm instruments, or wave ribbons as they sing and enjoy the music.

MORE EXPLORING:

Use these additional activities to extend the program or instead of the activity listed in Exploring.

Thanks for choosing our book for your Children's Church. We hope you and your children enjoy these celebrations of God's wonderful world!

Lisa Flinn and Barbara Younger

Hillsborough, North Carolina

COLORS in God's World

GREEN PASTURES

MESSAGE:
God gives us good things.

TWIRLING:
Ask the children to stand. Choose a child to spin the globe as you lead the children in **saying: Twirl and twirl God's wonderful world! Celebrate in Children's Church!** Next, ask everyone to twirl around once, then sit down.

SHARING:
Ask: Can you name something green that grows in God's world? *(Leaves on a tree. Grass. The herbs in my mother's garden.)*

LISTENING:
Plan on ending the story by leading children to a "green pasture." If there is a grassy area at your church, consider taking the children outdoors in good weather. If this won't work, spread out a green sheet or tablecloth in another part of the room, the hall, or another location inside the church. Disposable tablecloths are inexpensive and easy to find.

Say: **There is a Psalm in the Bible that speaks of the color green. Listen carefully as I read to you the 23rd Psalm.** Read Psalm 23.

Ask: **Does anyone remember the line that mentions the color green?** *(He makes me lie down in green pastures.)*

Say: **This Psalm is told through the eyes of a shepherd. A shepherd must find green pastures. The sheep need fresh, green grass for grazing. The green grass makes the sheep happy! For us, this verse helps us understand that**

BIBLE VERSE:

"HE MAKES ME LIE DOWN IN GREEN PASTURES."
(Psalm 23:2)

9

God of Our World,
thank you for
green pastures
and for everything
that grows green
in our world.
Thank you for the
good things of
life.
Amen.

COLORS

10

God will take us to green places too. Green places are the good things in life such as food and friends, rest and play, homes and happy times. Let's pretend we are shepherds leading our flock to a green pasture.

As you walk to the green pasture (taking a roundabout route if practical) point out streams, shady trees, and dangerous rocky ledges. Keep a lookout for sheep straying from the flock and wolves lurking in the distance. Wave to another shepherd. When you reach the green pasture, invite the children to lie down and relax for a few minutes. Then offer the prayer.

PRAYING:

Ask the children to close their eyes for a prayer.

EXPLORING:

To make Green Pasture Sponges, you will need sponges (one for every two children), grass seed, small plastic-coated bowls, tablespoons, and larger bowls for the grass seed and water. Before Children's Church, cut standard kitchen sponges in half. Place the grass seed in a bowl, with the tablespoons nearby, and fill another bowl with water.

Give a sponge and a plastic coated bowl to each child. Explain that they are going to grow a green pasture! Have them dip their sponges in the bowls of water, wring them out slightly, and place them in their bowls. Finally, have them sprinkle a generous spoonful of grass seed evenly over the sponges.

Explain to the children that their Green Pasture Sponges must stay wet and should be placed in a sunny window. Tell them to watch carefully for their green pastures to grow.

SNACKING:

Serve broccoli and celery with ranch dressing. To make the snack even greener, turn the dip green with a few drops of food coloring.

SINGING:

"The Lord Is My Shepherd"; "God Is so Good."

MORE EXPLORING:

To make a Green Pasture Patchwork, you will need sheets of white paper, crayons, and tape. Invite each child to color a green pasture. They may add any details they want such as sheep, children, rocks, rivers, and flowers. When the pastures are finished, have the children help you tape them together to create a patchwork of green pastures. Label the patchwork, "He makes me lie down in green pastures" and hang it in your church for everyone to admire.

COAT OF MANY COLORS

MESSAGE:

We celebrate the colors of God's world.

TWIRLING:

Ask the children to stand. Choose a child to spin the globe as you lead the children in **saying: Twirl and twirl God's wonderful world! Celebrate in Children's Church!** Next, ask everyone to twirl around once, then sit down.

SHARING:

Ask: What is the color of your favorite jacket or coat? *(Purple. Orange. Red.)*

LISTENING:

Make a Joseph Puppet to help you tell the story. The children will make their own Joseph Puppets in Exploring. You will need construction paper, fabric scraps in a variety of colors, scissors, glue, straws or craft sticks (tongue depressor size), tape, and crayons.

Begin by drawing, then cutting out the simple shape of a coat with Joseph's head at the top. Use crayons to give Joseph a mouth, nose, eyes, and hair. Tape the straw or craft stick to the bottom of the reverse side to create a handle. Using two-inch square fabric scraps, create a patchwork design on the jacket. Precut the puppets and fabric scraps for the children.

Hold up the Joseph Puppet as you have him tell the story.

Say: Hi everybody! Don't you just love my coat made with so many colors? (Pause, encouraging the children to answer.) **Do you have coats as beautiful as mine?** (Pause again for answers.) **My dad gave me mine. I am a character from the Bible. My name is Joseph. I have lots of brothers. My dad loves me the best. That's why he bought me this beautiful coat of many colors. Do you think it's fair for my dad to give me a beautiful coat because he loves me best?** (Pause for answers.) **Well it made my brothers very mad. They were so jealous. In fact they were so jealous that they ripped off my beautiful coat and threw me into a pit. Do you think that was very nice?** (Pause for answers.)

Well that's my story, and I don't have time to tell you about it today, but I ended up helping bring peace to my entire family. Is it good to bring peace to your family? (Pause for answers.)

BIBLE VERSE

"Now Israel loved Joseph more than any other of his children, because he was the son of his old age; and he had made him a long robe with sleeves."

(Genesis 37:3)

11

PRAY:

God of Our World,

we thank you for red hats,

(touch heads)

And Purple scarfs,

(pretend to throw scarf

around neck)

And green and blue

striped shirts,

(pretend to button shirt)

And blue jeans,

(run hands down legs)

And black socks,

(pretend to pull up socks)

And shoes that are silver

and orange.

(stamp feet)

Thanks God!

Colors

Today, I want you to remember something happy about my coat. My beautiful coat of many colors reminds us that God gave us wonderful colors. When we wear these colors, we are celebrating the colors of God's world. Now, you're going to make a Joseph Puppet and give him a beautiful coat too!

PRAYING:

Lead the children in the action prayer.

EXPLORING:

Hand a Joseph Puppet to each child. Invite him or her to draw his face, tape on the handle, then glue on the fabric squares. Explain that the squares may overlap. Set the finished puppets aside to dry.

SNACKING:

Serve a snack that Joseph might have enjoyed such as raisins, cheese, pita bread, and grapes. Explain to the children that these are foods that people ate in Bible times and foods we still enjoy today.

SINGING:

"Rise and Shine"; "I've Got Peace Like a River."

MORE EXPLORING:

Play the Stand Up Color Game. **Say: If you are wearing** (name a color), **stand up.** Name colors until all of the children are standing. To extend the game, play a few more rounds using these commands: **Stand up if you have a bathing suit or pajamas that are** (name colors); **Stand up if you have a hat, gloves, scarf, or boots that are** (name colors); **Stand up if you have a coat or jacket that is** (name colors.)

PURPLE CLOTH

MESSAGE:

We read about colors in the Bible.

TWIRLING:

Ask the children to stand. Choose a child to spin the globe as you lead the children in **saying: Twirl and twirl God's wonderful world! Celebrate in Children's Church!** Next, ask everyone to twirl around once, then sit down.

SHARING:

Ask: What is your favorite color? (*Aquamarine. Pink. Silver.*)

LISTENING:

For the story, the children will each need a strip of purple cloth to wave. If you can't locate purple cloth, they may each wave a strip of purple crepe paper streamer or purple paper.

Give each child a purple strip. **Say: This is your Purple Story Strip. Every time you hear the word "purple" in the story, wave your Purple Story Strip three times, then stop.**

Say: Colors are mentioned in many of the stories of the Bible. In one story, we learn about a woman named Lydia. Purple (pause) is important to her story. Paul, another person in the Bible, was a missionary who told everyone about Jesus.

One day, Paul traveled to Macedonia in Europe to tell the people there about Jesus. He noticed that the mountains of Macedonia looked purple (pause) in the distance. And he saw purple (pause) grapes growing on vines. At the market he noticed fish whose scales shimmered with purple (pause) scales. Then he spotted a woman who was selling fancy purple (pause) cloth. The woman selling the fancy purple (pause) cloth was Lydia. She sold the purple (pause) cloth to rich people.

Paul spoke to Lydia. He told her about Jesus. Lydia believed what Paul told her about Jesus and became a Christian. She invited Paul to stay in her home. Lydia was the first person in Europe to become a Christian. Some of the first church services in Europe were held in her home. Today, we remember Lydia because she helped Paul build the Christian Church in a new place. Hooray for Lydia and her purple (pause) cloth!

BIBLE VERSE: "A CERTAIN WOMAN NAMED LYDIA, A WORSHIPER OF GOD, WAS LISTENING TO US; SHE WAS FROM THE CITY OF THYATIRA AND A DEALER IN PURPLE CLOTH." (Acts 16:14)

13

PRAY:

God of Our World,
thank you for
Lydia,
who sold purple
cloth.
We're glad she
believed in Jesus
and helped Paul
build the
Christian Church
in a new place.
Amen.

PRAYING:

Ask the children to hold their purple strips against their hearts while you pray.

EXPLORING:

Play the Color Match Up Game. Before Children's Church, on separate sheets of paper, print each of these words in bold letters: RED, BLUE, PURPLE, WHITE, GREEN, YELLOW, BLACK, BROWN. Find objects in each of these colors. The kitchen and toy bin are good places to look.

Spread the color objects on the floor.

Say: Let's practice recognizing the color words for some of the colors in the Bible. One at a time, hand a child a color word. Have the child hold it up and let everyone join in calling out the word.

Tell the child to pick up the object in that color and hold it up high, then put it back down. Have the child give the color word back to you. Play until everyone has had at least one turn.

SNACKING:

In honor of Lydia, have the children use purple frosting to squirt the letter "P" onto graham crackers.

SINGING:

"Hallelu, Hallelu"; "I've Got Peace Like a River."

MORE EXPLORING:

Say: Just as we read about colors in the Bible, there are plenty of colors in our church too! Have children take turns *saying: I am thinking of something in our church that is (fill in a color.)* Then invite other children to guess what that something is. Depending on the age of your children, decide if the things they name need to be in sight or if they may be found anywhere in the church.

RAINBOW IN THE CLOUDS

MESSAGE:

God filled our world with color.

TWIRLING:

Ask the children to stand. Choose a child to spin the globe as you lead the children in **saying: Twirl and twirl God's wonderful world! Celebrate in Children's Church!** Next, ask everyone to twirl around once, then sit down.

SHARING:

Ask: Have you ever seen a rainbow? Where? *(At the beach. In a book. Last summer in my backyard.)*

LISTENING:

Teach the children the color wheel! Children will hop from color to color on a color wheel you create on the floor. You will need a sheet of red, orange, yellow, green, blue, and purple colored paper. If you don't have paper in these colors, you can color or paint white paper. Put each color a few feet apart, in a circle, in the order listed above. It's best to tape the paper to the floor to keep it from moving when the children hop onto it.

Say: A long time ago God told a good man named Noah that a huge storm was coming. Noah built a big boat that kept his family and a lot of animals safe. When the storm was over, God told him to bring his family and the animals outside and look at the sky. God set a rainbow in the clouds as a promise that the whole world would never be destroyed again by a flood.

Ask: In the story of Noah and the Ark, what appears in the sky when the flood is over? *(A rainbow.)*

Say: When we see a rainbow in the sky, we are to remember God's promise. We also remember that God has filled our world with beautiful colors.

A color wheel shows us these colors in this order: red, orange, yellow, green, blue, purple. Today I made a color wheel on the floor. You're each going to get to take a turn hopping from color to color as we say the colors together.

Let the children take turns hopping from color to color as you lead the group in repeating the colors with each hop.

BIBLE VERSE:

"I have set my bow in the clouds, and it shall be a sign of the covenant between me and the earth."

(Genesis 9:13)

15

PRAY:

God of Our World,

thank you for red,

orange, yellow, green,

blue, and purple, and all

of the other colors too,

we thank you!

Amen.

PRAYING:

Have the children form a wide circle around the color wheel. **Pray.**

EXPLORING:

The children will make Color Wheels. You will need white paper plates, crayons, and a ruler. Before Children's Church, using a black or brown crayon, divide the plates into six sections, as if dividing a pie. Use a crayon in the correct color to make a dot of color in each section in this order: red, orange, yellow, green, blue, and purple.

Lead the children in coloring each section the appropriate color. When the Color Wheels are finished, have the children wave them in the air. Ask them to *say after you: Thank you, God, for the colors of your world!*

SNACKING:

Spread out a rainbow of cool pops. Admire the wonderful colors, then let the children choose a cool pop.

SINGING:

"Who Built the Ark?" "Dance and Sing, for the Lord Is With Us."

MORE EXPLORING:

Play Color Call Out. **Say: God filled our world with color. Let's call out the colors of God's World. I'll say a category, and you call out things in that category and what color they are.** For example, you will **call out: animals,** and the children will *call out: orange tigers, gray elephants, and red foxes.* Other categories can be Flowers, Birds, Vegetables, Fruits, and Bugs.

COLORS

RED MITTENS

MESSAGE:

God sends beautiful snow.

TWIRLING:

Ask the children to stand. Choose a child to spin the globe as you lead the children in **saying: Twirl and twirl God's wonderful world! Celebrate in Children's Church!** Next, ask everyone to twirl around once, then sit down.

SHARING:

Ask: Can you tell us about a time when you enjoyed being in the snow? *(My brother and I went sledding. I built a snowman with my cousin. Last winter when we had the blizzard.)* If you live in an area where it doesn't snow, ask the children what they think they would enjoy doing in the snow.

LISTENING:

To tell the story, you will snip a cloud, a snowflake, a pair of mittens, and a snowman. Practice doing this. To cut the cloud, fold a sheet of paper in half. Cut a semi-circle with scalloped edges. To cut a snowflake, fold a sheet of paper into a small rectangle. Make deep triangular snips along all four sides. To cut a snowman, fold a sheet of paper in half and cut three connecting semi-circles, each a bit smaller than the next. To cut the mittens, fold a sheet of paper in half. Starting with the thumb at the fold line, cut the shape of a mitten. Cut the thumb so it is no longer attached to the fold. You may want to sketch the outline for the snowman and mittens ahead of time. Plan on using white paper for the cloud, snowflake and snowman. Use red paper for the mittens.

Say: Even in Bible times, God sent beautiful snow! There's a verse in the Bible that talks about a woman being ready for snow, because she had crimson clothing for her family to put on. This was probably a sort of wool which was a deep red in color. Today, God sends beautiful snow too. Listen to Jessica's story:

Jessica looked up and saw a puffy (cut out the cloud and hold it up) **cloud in the sky. "I hope it's going to snow," she said to her friend. "I love it when God sends us beautiful snow!" Just then, Jessica noticed a white** (cut snowflake and hold up) **snowflake floating slowly to the ground. In a few minutes, the snow was coming faster and faster. "Let's make a cool** (cut out snowman and hold it up) **snowman," said Jessica.**

17

BiBLe VeRSe:

"SHe iS NoT AFRAiD FoR HeR HouSeHoLD WHeN iT SNoWS, FoR ALL HeR HouSeHoLD iS CLoTHeD iN CRiMSoN."

(Proverbs 31:21)

COLORS

18

Just then her mother rushed out with two pairs of warm red (cut out the mittens and hold them up) **mittens for Jessica and her friend. Before long, they had made a cool** (hold up snowman) **snowman with the beautiful** (hold up snowflake) **snowflakes that came from the puffy** (hold up cloud) **cloud. "I'm glad God sends us beautiful snow," said Jessica. "Me too," said her friend, "and I'm glad your mother brought us warm red** (hold up mittens) **mittens.**

PRAYiNG:

Have children hold their hands high in the air, then gradually move them down, wiggling fingers to create falling snowflakes as you pray.

eXPLoRiNG:

To make Red Mitten Ornaments, you will need paper, red felt squares, scissors, yarn, stapler or hole punch, and white or silver glitter glue pens or glitter and glue. Plan on cutting four mittens from each felt square.

Before Children's Church, make the pattern of a mitten on paper, about the size of one quarter of the felt square. Cut two mittens for each child. Staple a six-inch length of yarn between two mittens to form a hanger or use a hole punch to punch a hole in each mitten, then tie one end of the yarn to each mitten.

Say: In honor of the beautiful snow that God sends to our world, you're going to make Red Mitten Ornaments to hang on your Christmas tree or anywhere else you would like. We'll use glitter that looks like snow to decorate the mittens. Have the children decorate their mittens with glitter.

SNACKiNG:

Make Beautiful Snow Cookies. Bake or purchase chocolate or spice cookies. Put confectioner's sugar into a shaker, strainer, or sifter and let the children sprinkle their cookies with sugar snow.

SiNGiNG:

"My God Is so Great"; "Rejoice in the Lord Always."

MoRe eXPLoRiNG:

Lead the children through this action song, sung to the tune of "This Is the Way We Wash Our Clothes":

This is the way we throw a snowball, throw a snowball, throw a snowball. This is the way we throw a snowball in God's beautiful snow. (Pretend to pack, then throw a snowball.)

This is the way we build a snowman, build a snowman, build a snowman. This is the way we build a snowman in God's beautiful snow. (Pretend to roll a large ball of snow, then lift it onto the snowman.)

This is the way we glide and slip, glide and slip, glide and slip. This is the way we glide and slip in God's beautiful snow. (Pretend to glide, then slip.)

This is the way we twirl in the snow, twirl in the snow, twirl in the snow. This is the way we twirl in the snow, in God's beautiful snow. (Spread arms and twirl around.)

This is the way we taste the snowflakes, taste the snowflakes, taste the snowflakes. This is the way we taste the snowflakes in God's beautiful snow. (Tilt head upwards and stick out tongue.)

Encourage the children to help you create more snowy lyrics and motions.

PRAY:
God of Our World, thank you for sending beautiful, beautiful snow. Amen.

PRAY:

God of Our World, thank you for giving us delicious foods in many colors.
We thank you for red strawberries and orange sherbet and green celery and purple plums and blue gelatin and yellow lemon drops and cupcakes with sprinkles in lots of colors.
Amen.

WHITE MANNA

MESSAGE:

God gives us food in many colors.

TWIRLING:

Ask the children to stand. Choose a child to spin the globe as you lead the children in **saying: Twirl and twirl God's wonderful world! Celebrate in Children's Church!** Next, ask everyone to twirl around once, then sit down.

SHARING:

Ask: Can you tell us one of your favorite foods? *(Pizza. Chocolate chip cookies. Macaroni and cheese.)*

LISTENING:

Tell the children the story of the Israelites and the manna.

Say: In the Bible, we learn about Moses. Moses led the Israelites out of Egypt to the Holy Land. To get to the Holy Land, they had to cross the desert. They got very hungry so God sent them a special food to eat. They found this food on the ground. Listen to a verse that tells us about the special food. Read the Bible Verse. **God gives us food too. Our food isn't just white, like the manna, but it comes in many colors. Let's go around and name a food, then tell what color it is.** (Let the children take turns naming foods and telling their colors.)

PRAYING:

Ask the children to picture each food in their mind as you pray. Say the foods slowly to give children a few seconds to visualize them.

EXPLORING:

Have the children make a colorful table runner for your next church fellowship event. You will need shelf or craft paper and crayons. If you don't have a length of paper, simply tape sheets of paper together.

Spread out the length of paper. Let the children watch you as you print down the center, "Thank you, God, for colorful foods!" Invite them to use crayons to decorate the table runner with their favorite colorful foods. If they have trouble thinking of foods, here are some to suggest: grapes, bananas, pizza, strawberries, watermelon, lemons, apples, cupcakes with sprinkles, hot-dogs, ice cream cones, and broccoli.

Use the table runner to add color to an upcoming fellowship event such as a coffee hour or a church supper.

SNACKING:

Serve the children yogurt or vanilla pudding. Invite them to stir in a spoonful of colorful sprinkles.

SINGING:

"My God Is so Great"; "Dance and Sing for the Lord Will Be With Us."

MORE EXPLORING:

Take the children on a Colorful Candy Hunt! Before Children's Church, hide individually wrapped candies. When it's time for the hunt, remind children that the Israelites found manna on the ground in the desert. Suggest that there just might be some candy for your Children's Church kids to find! You may want to set a limit of how many candies each child may pick up.

BIBLE VERSE:

"The house of Israel called it manna; it was like coriander seed, white, and the taste of it was like wafers made with honey."

(Exodus 16:31)

PRAY:

God of Our
World,
we think you
were very smart
to make the
wonderful sun
that lights up
the world for
everyone.
Good thinking,
God!
Amen.

THE YELLOW SUN

MESSAGE:

God made the sun to bring light, warmth, and color to the world.

TWIRLING:

Ask the children to stand. Choose a child to spin the globe as you lead the children in **saying: Twirl and twirl God's wonderful world! Celebrate in Children's Church!** Next, ask everyone to twirl around once, then sit down.

SHARING:

Ask: What is something you like to do outdoors on a sunny day? *(I like to swing on my swing. It's cool to ride my bike. Sit on my porch and read.)*

LISTENING:

Begin by holding up the Bible. **Ask: What book is this?** *(The Bible.)*

Say: We learn a lot about God's world in the Bible. In the first book of the Bible, the book of Genesis, we learn how God created the world. These verses tell of God creating the sun and the moon and stars.
      Read Genesis 1:14-19.

Say: On the fourth day of creation, God made the sun. The sun gives energy and warmth to the world; causes plants to grow; and gives light. Without light, we would not be able to see any colors in God's world.

Ask the children to each name one or two things in God's world that they especially like to see.

PRAYING:

Have the children hold their arms in a circle above their heads. **Say: Pretend this circle is the wonderful sun. Hold up the sun as I pray.**

EXPLORING:

To make Sunny Sun Visors you will need white paper plates, crayons, scissors, stapler, and elastic. Cut paper plates in half. Staple lengths of elastic about six inches long to both ends of the straight side of the visor. Decorate a sample visor with a sunny design.

Give each child a visor, then show them your sample. Explain that even though the sun is one of God's most important creations, we need to be careful that we protect our eyes and skin from the sun. Sun visors help us to do this. When the visors are finished, have the children model them for you.

SNACKING:

Serve the children a scoop of orange or yellow ice cream or sherbet in honor of the sun.

SINGING:

"Climb, Climb Up Sunshine Mountain"; "Joyful, Joyful, We Adore Thee."

MORE EXPLORING:

To make Sunny Day Puzzles you will need paper, crayons, and scissors. Have the children color bright suns that fill their pages. Then ask them to cut their pictures into four puzzle pieces. Let them switch puzzles with other children and have fun putting the Sunny Day Puzzles together again.

BIBLE VERSE:

"God made the two great lights—the greater light to rule the day and the lesser light to rule the night."

(Genesis 1:16)

CREATURES in God's World

BIBLE VERSE:

"Then the king gave the command, and Daniel was brought and thrown into the den of lions."

(Daniel 6:16)

WILD THINGS

MESSAGE:

There are wild animals in God's world.

TWIRLING:

Ask the children to stand. Choose a child to spin the globe as you lead the children in **saying: Twirl and twirl God's wonderful world! Celebrate in Children's Church!** Next, ask everyone to twirl around once, then sit down.

SHARING:

Ask: What is your favorite wild animal? *(Lions. Rhinos. Gorillas.)*

LISTENING:

As you tell the story of Daniel, have the children *shout: Roar* every time they hear the word "lion" or "lions." Practice this a few times.

Say: In the Book of Daniel, we learn about a man named "Daniel" who was thrown into a lions' (pause: roar) den. How scary it must have been for Daniel to be thrown into a lions' (pause: roar) den! This is what happened.

Daniel became friends with King Darius. This made the officials of his kingdom jealous. They tried to come up with a way to get Daniel into trouble. The King passed a rule that no one could pray to God. They could only pray to the King. Daniel loved God, and so he continued to pray. When the King found this out, he was very sad. He didn't want to punish Daniel. But he had to because Daniel had broken the law. With a sad heart, the King had Daniel thrown into the lions' (pause: roar) den. As he did, he said to Daniel, "May your God, whom you faithfully serve, save you!"

Poor Daniel. There he was in the den with the lions (pause: roar.) The next day, the King went to check on Daniel. He called to him in the lions' (pause: roar) den, "Daniel has your God saved you?" Daniel called back from the lions' (pause: roar) den, "My God sent an angel to shut the mouths of the lions (pause: roar) so they could not hurt me." The King was happy that Daniel was safe and that God had saved him. He commanded that Daniel be taken out of the lions' (pause: roar) den. Daniel's faith in God kept him safe from the lions (pause: roar.)

PRAYING:

Say: As we understand from the story of Daniel, we must be careful around wild animals. They can be dangerous. But wild animals are wonderful creatures too, and an important part of God's world. Have the children repeat each line of the prayer after you.

EXPLORING:

To make Lion Masks you will need plain paper plates with fluted edges, a pencil, crayons, and scissors. When it's time to model the masks, you can simply have the children hold up their masks to their faces, attach a straw or craft stick (tongue depressor size) handle with tape, or staple a length of elastic to the sides.

Before Children's Church, use a pencil to draw the face of a lion in the center of each plate. Make a triangle for a nose and round eyes. Add the outline of a mouth, whiskers, and ears. If you wish, cut out the eyes so the children can see through the mask.

When it's time to make the masks, invite the children to darken the outline of the mouth, whiskers, and ears with crayon. Next have them color the nose and eyes in a dark shade and the rest of the lion's face brown, tan, yellow, or orange. Finally, show them how to cut into the fluted edge to create a fringed mane. Have the children model their lion masks for one another and encourage them to roar their loudest roar in a wild things dance!

SNACKING:

Serve Jungle Juice with a Banana Stirrer. Slice bananas and put two or three slices on a straw. Place the Banana Stirrers into cups, then pour in juice. Explain to the children that bananas are often found in jungles, where many of God's wild animals live.

SINGING:

"Who Did Swallow Jonah?" "When I Am Afraid."

PRAY:

We thank you, God, for animals of the wild. Those who are ferocious and those who are mild. Amen.

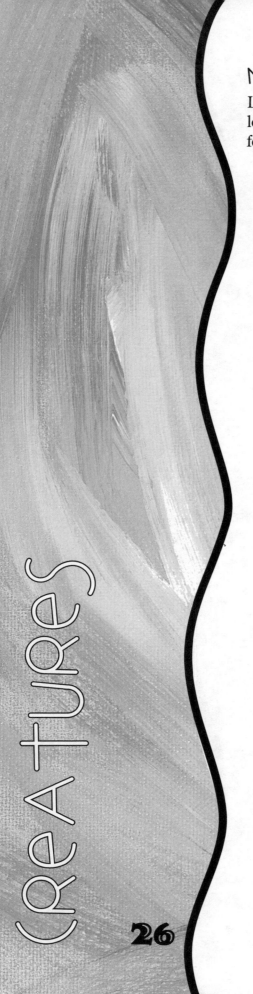

MORE EXPLORING:

Let the children take turns leading a Wild Animals Parade. The leader will mimic the behavior of an animal and everyone else will follow those actions. Here are some suggestions:

Gorillas: Stoop over, hang arms low and swing.

Lions: Turn head from side to side and roar.

Giraffes: Walk with neck held high and stiff legs.

Elephants: Lumber slowly, swinging one arm as a trunk, with the other arm behind back.

Monkey: Bop along, scratching ribs.

Kangaroo: Hop with arms bent against chest, fingers turned down.

SLITHERING SNAKES

MESSAGE:
There were snakes even in Bible times.

TWIRLING:
Ask the children to stand. Choose a child to spin the globe as you lead the children in **saying: Twirl and twirl God's wonderful world! Celebrate in Children's Church!** Next, ask everyone to twirl around once, then sit down.

SHARING:
Ask: Have you ever seen a snake? *(In my grandpa's basement. When I went on a hike with my uncle. I saw a boa constrictor and lots of other snakes at the zoo.)*

LISTENING:
To assist you, create a snake puppet friend, Samuel, from a sock. Use a marker to give him eyes and a tongue. Put your hand in Samuel and let him tell the story. As Samuel talks, add plenty of "sssss" sounds to his speech.

Say: Sssssssssssss. Salutations! I'm Samuel. And I've slithered up from Bible times to tell you about snakes who slither in the pages of the Bible. You can read about a snake early on, the snake from the Garden of Eden who tempted Eve to eat from the forbidden tree. You can read about snakes in the story of Moses and snakes in the Book of Psalms and snakes in the story of Job. Sometimes in the Bible we snakes are called "serpents." In the New Testament, Paul gets bitten by a snake and in the last book of the Bible, Revelations, you read about snakes too.

We slithered lots in Bible times just as we do today. Some people are afraid of snakes and yes, we can be dangerous, but we snakes are marvelous too. We are splendid, smashing, sensational, and stunning creatures in God's amazing world. Sssssssssss. See ya!

PRAYING:
Let each child take a turn putting on Samuel and making him *say:* (with plenty of "ssss") *Snakes are stunning!"* Then ask them to close their eyes and bow their heads. **Pray.**

BIBLE VERSE:
"Now the serpent was more crafty than any other wild animal that the Lord God had made."

(Genesis 3:1)

PRAY:
God of Our World, from reading the Bible, we understand that snakes were a part of your world in Bible times too. Thank you for all the splendid, smashing, sensational, and stunning creatures who grace your earth. Amen.

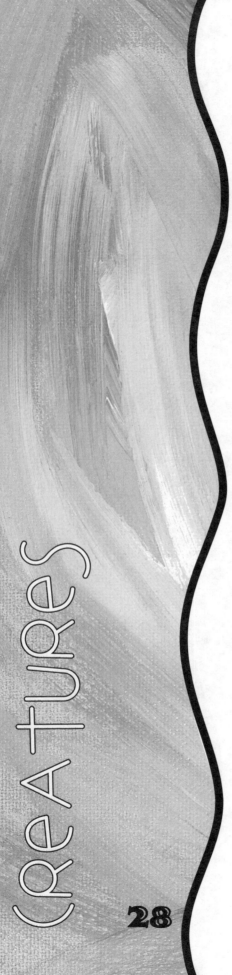

EXPLORING:

To make Spiraling Snakes, you will need plain paper plates, pencil, scissors, and crayons. Consider bringing in a book that has color drawings or photographs of snakes.

Cut and color a sample snake to show the children. Make a diagonal cut (this will be the snake's tail) about one-and-a-half inches into the paper plate. (Smooth this edge when you are finished cutting the spiral.) Continue cutting in a spiraling fashion to the center (this is the snake's head.) Fold the head in half so the head pops up. Color the snake a bright pattern. If you think your children will have trouble cutting the snakes, you may want to do this ahead of time. If not, use a pencil to mark cutting lines for them. It's a good idea to have extra paper plates in case children make mistakes in cutting.

Begin by showing the children the snake book if you have one, pointing out the tremendous variety of snake colors and patterns. Next, show the children how to cut their own Spiraling Snakes. Then invite them to decorate their snakes. When finished, have everyone hold up their squiggling serpents!

SNACKING:

Children will love to squirt snakes onto graham crackers using canned squirt cheese. Suggest they create a squiggling snake on one cracker and a coiled snake on another.

SINGING:

"Rejoice in the Lord Always"; "When I Am Afraid."

MORE EXPLORING:

Lead the children in these Snakey Tongue Twisters. As they master each one, have them say it faster and faster:

Squiggly snakes slither slowly in the summer grass.

Scaly striped snakes slip silently into the stream.

Some snakes simply love to slither through the swamp.

Stunning and stupendous snakes shout, "Snakes are super cool!"

LOVING PETS

MESSAGE:
We love God's animals.

TWIRLING:
Ask the children to stand. Choose a child to spin the globe as you lead the children in **saying: Twirl and twirl God's wonderful world! Celebrate in Children's Church!** Next, ask everyone to twirl around once, then sit down.

SHARING:
Ask: Can you tell us about a pet you have or would like to have? *(I have two golden retrievers. We have a cat named "Rufus." I want to get a guinea pig.)*

LISTENING:
Use two poems about a lamb to help children think about loving pets.

Ask: There's a famous poem about a girl who loved her pet lamb. What's the name of the poem? *(Mary Had a Little Lamb.)*

Say: Let's say the poem together:

> Mary had a little lamb.
>
> Its fleece was white as snow.
>
> And everywhere that Mary went,
>
> The lamb was sure to go.

Continue: There's a story about a pet lamb in the Bible, too. Here's a poem about that lamb:

> There's a story in the Bible about a little lamb,
>
> Who was loved oh so much by a poor man.
>
> He brought her home and cared for her,
>
> And treated her like a daughter.
>
> He shared his food and his cup,
>
> And every day he picked her up!

Read the rhyme again, asking the children to repeat each line after you.

Conclude by **saying: God has given us pets to love. What a wonderful part of God's wonderful world!**

BIBLE VERSE:
"BUT THE POOR MAN HAD NOTHING BUT ONE LITTLE EWE LAMB, WHICH HE HAD BOUGHT."
(2 Samuel 12:3)

29

PRAY:

God of Our World, thank you for giving us animals to love. We thank you especially for the animal we are picturing in our minds right now (pause.) Amen.

CREATURES

PRAYING:

Ask the children to picture an animal they have loved when you pause during the prayer. Have them to bow their heads and close their eyes. **Pray.**

EXPLORING:

Children will have fun creating animals out of play clay to display in a pretend pet show. Purchase dough or use the following recipe to make your own:

To make Play Clay, mix two cups flour, one cup salt, and four teaspoons cream of tartar in a saucepan. To one cup water, add two Tablespoons of cooking oil and several drops of food coloring. Add the wet ingredients to the saucepan and stir. Cook over medium heat until the mixture begins to pull away from the sides of the pan and forms a ball. Cool, then knead. Store in an airtight container. This recipe should yield enough modeling dough for about ten children.

Invite the children to create a pet for the pretend pet show. Encourage them to think of all sorts of pets from dogs and cats to tropical fish and guinea pigs to parrots and rabbits. When the pets are finished, line them up on a table. Have the children introduce their pets, say their pet's name, and something special about their pets.

SNACKING:

For a silly snack, serve a favorite dry cereal in small bowls. Tell the children that they are snacking on pretend kitty or puppy chow.

SINGING:

"God's Love"; "Praise the Lord of All Creation."

MORE EXPLORING:

Read a picture book about a pet such as Steven Kellogg's, *Can I Keep Him* or *Pinkerton, Behave!* Gene Zion's, *Harry the Dirty Dog* Books. Or Holly Keller's, *Goodbye, Max.*

ANIMAL HOMES

MESSAGE:
In God's world, animals have homes.

TWIRLING:
Ask the children to stand. Choose a child to spin the globe as you lead the children in **saying: Twirl and twirl God's wonderful world! Celebrate in Children's Church!** Next, ask everyone to twirl around once, then sit down.

SHARING:
Ask: Have you ever seen a bird's nest? *(We found one in our Christmas tree last year. At school we have one in our Science Center. My cousin found one in his barn.)*

LISTENING:
During the story, children will play the roll of a bird flying about building a nest. Have the children practice flapping their wings. Tell them that they are to flap their wings three times whenever they hear the word, "fly."

Say: I am a mother bird. I need to build a nest where I can lay my eggs. I've chosen this tree branch as the best place to build my nest. Now I must fly (pause) **around and look for materials. Whenever I find something, I'll bring it back to this branch. Since I am a bird called a Baltimore Oriole, I like to build my nest out of lots of materials.**

I see some twigs. I'll fly (pause) **down and get those. There are some stalks of grass in that field. I'll fly** (pause) **down and get those too. Oh good! I see some string over there on the ground. I'll fly** (pause) **down and pick it up. There's a long piece of yarn hanging from that low branch. I'll fly** (pause) **and get that next. Great! There's a clump of hair from some-one's hairbrush. I'll fly** (pause) **over near the porch and get that. Now I'll fly** (pause) **down and get some more grass. This nest is really coming along! What a wonderful nest for my babies. I'm glad God gave animals the ability to make their own homes.**

PRAYING:
Ask the children to touch the fingers of one hand to the other to create a pretend bird's nest. **Pray.**

31

PRAY:

God of Our
World,
thank you for
helping birds
build the nests
they like the best!
Amen.

EXPLORING:

To make Birdy Treats, you will need pine cones or toasted bread slices, peanut butter or shortening, birdseed, string, scissors, knives, a pan, and food storage bags. Before Children's Church, pour the birdseed into a shallow pan. Cut lengths of string to be hangers for the Birdy Treats.

Say: There's a verse in the Bible that talks about birds who nested at the Temple. (Read the verse.) **There are birds who live near our church, too. Today, we're going to make a treat for those birds and a treat for you to give to the birds who live near your homes.**

Demonstrate how to spread peanut butter or shortening onto the pine cone or bread slice, then roll it in birdseed. Attach a yarn hanger by tying it around the pine cone or poking a small hole in the bread and looping the hanger through it. Next, have the children create their own Birdy Treats. When the treats are finished, put each one in a food storage bag.

If possible, take the children outside to help hang the demonstration Birdy Treat. If this isn't practical, promise you will hang it later. Send the children's Birdy Treats home with them, explaining that they are to hang the treats for the birds who nest near their homes.

SNACKING:

Show the children how to arrange dry chow mien noodles on a paper plate to create a bird's nest. Give them each a few jelly beans to put into their nests. Admire the lovely nests before you invite children to enjoy them for a snack.

SINGING:

"He's Got the Whole World"; "Praise the Lord, All Creation."

MORE EXPLORING:

Celebrate the names of other animals and their homes with these lyrics, sung to "The Farmer in the Dell:"

The fox lives in a den.
The fox lives in a den.
Thank you, God, for animal homes.
The fox lives in a den.
The spider lives in a web...
The beaver lives in a lodge...
The bee lives in a hive...
The wombat lives in a burrow...
The rabbit lives in a warren...
The mole lives in a hole...

BUSY ANTS

MESSAGE:

In God's world, everyone has a job to do.

TWIRLING:

Ask the children to stand. Choose a child to spin the globe as you lead the children in **saying: Twirl and twirl God's wonderful world! Celebrate in Children's Church!** Next, ask everyone to twirl around once, then sit down.

SHARING:

Ask: Do you have a job or chore you do to help around the house? *(I feed my cat. I bring in the mail. I sweep the porch.)*

LISTENING:

Begin by asking the children some questions about ants.

Ask: Where do you usually see ants? Do they ever come into your house? What color ants have you seen? What size ants have you seen? What are the ants doing when you see them? Have you seen ants marching in a long line? What do you think is interesting about ants?

Say: Ants live all over God's world, except in the very cold climates. Ants live together in colonies. These colonies have worker ants who do all sort of jobs. Worker ants build nests by carving tunnels in the ground or carrying twigs, pine needles, and dirt to build mounds. Some ants chew into wood to make nests and some construct nests using tree leaves. Worker ants gather food for their colonies. Some ants collect seeds to store and others gather honeydew from plants. And maybe you've seen worker ants carrying a cookie crumb from your own kitchen floor! These worker ants have important jobs to do for their colonies. In God's world, even insects have jobs to do!

PRAYING:

Say: When we all work to do our jobs, it makes God's world a better place. There's a verse in the Bible that tells us to take note of how hard ants work. Read the Bible verse. **Say:** This verse is telling us to be good workers like the ant. Ask the children to bow their heads and close their eyes. Pray.

BIBLE VERSE:

"Go to the ant, you lazybones; consider its ways, and be wise."

(Proverbs 6:6)

PRAY:

God of Our
World,
we don't want to
be
lazybones!
Help us to be
good workers just
like the ants.
Amen.

EXPLORING:

To create Crazy Ants, you will need regular or desert size white paper plates, chenille stems, a hole punch, stapler and crayons. Make a sample Crazy Ant to show the children. Staple three paper plates together to form the body of the ant. Choose one end to be the head and color two dark eyes. Punch two holes at the end of the head and twist two chenille stems through the holes to form antennae. Color the ant with vibrant colors in a fun pattern. Consider stapling the plates together and punching the holes ahead of time if your group is large or you think your children may have trouble with this task. Hold up your Crazy Ant.

Say: In the ant world, most ants are brown, black, or rust colored; but some are green, yellow, blue, or purple. Today you're going to make Crazy Ants. You can color your ants with any colors you like in any sort of crazy pattern. When the ants are finished, line them up on the floor in an ant parade.

SNACKING:

Serve Busy Ants Cupcakes! Top cupcakes with chocolate sprinkles.

SINGING:

"God's Love"; "Praise the Lord, All Creation."

MORE EXPLORING:

Teach the children the song, "The Ants Go Marching" to the tune of "When Johnny Comes Marching Home Again":

The ants go marching one by one, hurrah, hurrah.
The ants go marching one by one, hurrah, hurrah.
The ants go marching one by one.
The little one stops to suck his thumb,
And they all go marching down into the ground,
to get out of the rain.

The ants go marching two by two, hurrah, hurrah.
The ants go marching two by two, hurrah, hurrah.
The ants go marching two by two.
The little one stops to tie his shoe,
And they all go marching down into the ground,
to get out of the rain.

The ants go marching three by three, hurrah, hurrah.
The ants go marching three by three, hurrah, hurrah.
The ants go marching three by three.
The little one stops to climb a tree,
And they all go marching down into the ground,
to get out of the rain.

SEA CREATURES

MESSAGE:
God created sea creatures great and small.

TWIRLING:
Ask the children to stand. Choose a child to spin the globe as you lead the children in **saying: Twirl and twirl God's wonderful world! Celebrate in Children's Church!** Next, ask everyone to twirl around once, then sit down.

SHARING:
Ask: Can you name a creature that lives in the seas? (*A sea horse. A blue whale. A giant squid.*)

LISTENING:
Before Children's Church, color a large octopus on a piece of posterboard or craft paper. Add a few small sea creatures such as a rainbow fish and a sea horse. Cut the poster into four or five pieces. Have clear tape at hand. If you can find a book that has photographs or illustrations of sea creatures, bring that along too.

Show the children the puzzle pieces. **Say: I need helpers to piece our puzzle together.** Call two children forward. After they have put the puzzle together, use tape to secure it. Thank the children and tell them to be seated. Hold up the puzzle and **ask: What do you see?**

Say: This big creature is a giant octopus. (Say the names of the smaller creatures.) **When God created the world, God filled the seas with giant sea creatures, tiny sea creatures, and all of the sizes in between! The seas are amazing places, filled with amazing creatures great and small.**

If you have a book of sea creatures, show this to the children now. If not, spend some time talking with them about some of the amazing creatures in the sea.

PRAYING:
Bags of seashells can be purchased in many craft, hobby, or science stores. Give each child a shell to hold. If you weren't able to locate sea shells, ask the children to cup one hand into the other, pretending they are holding a shell. Explain that some sea creatures live in shells. **Pray.**

PRAY:
God of Our World,
we thank you for sea creatures great and small.
Amen.

BIBLE VERSE:

"So God created the great sea monsters."

(Genesis 1:21)

EXPLORING:

To make a Sea Creatures Book, you will need paper, crayons, scissors, and a stapler. Before Children's Church, assemble the books. Cut paper in half vertically. Place one cut sheet of paper on top of the other and fold in half to form a book. Staple twice down the outside of the fold. Write "SEA CREATURES" on each cover in colorful letters.

Give each child a blank book. **Say: This book is going to become your very own book of sea creatures. Color a different sea creature on each page to create a book filled with amazing sea creatures, great and small.**

When they are finished, have the children take turns showing their books to the group.

SNACKING:

Children love gummy treats. Look for gummy fish, but if you can't find them, gummy worms can become sea snakes and eels!

SINGING:

"God's Love"; "Praise the Lord All Creation."

MORE EXPLORING:

Read to the children the refrain to "All Things Bright and Beautiful":

> All things bright and beautiful,
>
> All creatures great and small,
>
> All things wise and wonderful;
>
> The Lord God made them all.

Explain that this verse is from a poem written by a woman named Cecil Frances Alexander. The poem was set to music and first published over one hundred and fifty years ago in a hymnal for children. If you are familiar with the tune to this beloved hymn, lead the children in singing it. Then let children each take a turn naming a great creature and a small creature that they especially like.

FARM ANIMALS

MESSAGE:

Farms have animals too.

TWIRLING:

Ask the children to stand. Choose a child to spin the globe as you lead the children in **saying: Twirl and twirl God's wonderful world! Celebrate in Children's Church!** Next, ask everyone to twirl around once, then sit down.

SHARING:

Ask: Can you name a farm animal that you really like? *(Pigs. Chicken. Llamas.)*

LISTENING:

Ask the children these riddles. After they guess each animal, invite them to make the sound that animal makes.

Ask: Who has a curly tale and loves to roll in mud? *(A pig.)*

Who has a woolly fleece? *(A sheep.)*

Who helps keep mice out of the barn? *(A cat.)*

Who likes to eat grass and chew and chew? *(A cow.)*

Who wears shoes and a saddle? *(A Horse.)*

Who wakes up the farm? *(A rooster.)*

Who lays eggs? *(A chicken.)*

Who helps protect the farm? *(A dog.)*

Say: These are some of the animals that live on a farm. Since Bible times, farm animals have helped farmers produce food. Farm animals are important creatures in God's world.

PRAYING:

Sing the prayer based on the tune of "Old McDonald Had a Farm."

EXPLORING:

Play Farm Animal Scramble. Draw simple pictures of a pig, sheep, chicken, and cow on separate sheets of paper. Before Children's Church, tape the pictures to different walls.

To play, explain to the children that you will make the sound of one of the animals on the walls. When they hear the sound, they are to start making the sound too and run (or hurry) to the picture of the

PRAY:

Thank you, God, for all farm animals, e-i-e-i-o. With a neigh, neigh here; and a moo, moo there, here an oink, there a meow, everywhere a cock-a-doodle-doo. Thank you, God, for all farm animals, e-i-e-i-o. Amen.

BIBLE VERSE:

"HE HAD POSSESSIONS OF FLOCKS AND HERDS."

(Genesis 26:14)

animal who makes the sound. Do several rounds, scrambling the order of the animals. Then let the children take turns calling out the sounds.

SNACKING:

Serve Brown and White Cows by adding a scoop of chocolate ice cream to a glass of regular milk or a scoop of vanilla ice cream to a glass of chocolate milk.

SINGING:

"God's Love"; "Praise the Lord, All Creation."

MORE EXPLORING:

Inexpensive packs of plastic farm animals can be purchased in toy departments. Children will love receiving them as a small gift to take home. Consider creating one or several farm play boards on posterboard. Draw roads, a pond, a barn, and fields. Children can have fun moving their farm animals around the farm. Consider, too, leading the children in "Old MacDonald Had a Farm," asking them to hold up their animals when they hear that animal named in the song.

GARDENS
in God's World

SHARING FOOD

MESSAGE:

We share food with those who are hungry.

TWIRLING:

Ask the children to stand. Choose a child to spin the globe as you lead the children in **saying: Twirl and twirl God's wonderful world! Celebrate in Children's Church!** Next, ask everyone to twirl around once, then sit down.

SHARING:

Ask: When you are really hungry, what food do you want the most? *(Spaghetti. Cereal. Grapes.)*

LISTENING:

Take the children on a pretend tour of a food pantry or food bank. (Before or after the story, you may want to give some details about organizations in your community that assist those in need of food.)

Say: Many people in our church and community buy extra food when they shop for groceries. They give this extra food to a place called a "food pantry" or a "food bank." The food pantry gives food to people who cannot afford to buy food for their families. Let's take a pretend tour of the food pantry. Listen carefully as I describe it to you.

As we go in the front door, we see a few people standing in line at the counter. These people are waiting to receive some

BIBLE VERSE:

"THEY ALSO GAVE HIM A PIECE OF FIG CAKE AND TWO CLUSTERS OF RAISINS. WHEN HE HAD EATEN, HIS SPIRIT REVIVED; FOR HE HAD NOT EATEN BREAD OR DRUNK WATER FOR THREE DAYS AND THREE NIGHTS."

(I Samuel 30:12)

39

PRAY:

God of Our World, thank you for good food to share and for all the people who care for the hungry. Amen.

needed food. Behind the counter, we see several people filling grocery bags with boxes, cans, and jars.

We go through a door into a large room that is set up like a small grocery store. Everything is lined up on shelves. We see cans of ham, tuna, chicken, corned beef, and chili. There are boxes of cereal, macaroni and cheese, spaghetti, crackers, cake mixes, granola bars, tea, and pancake mixes.

We see bags of sugar, flour, coffee, cornmeal, dried fruit, rice, noodles, and muffin mixes. There are jars of peanut butter, jelly, spaghetti sauce, gravy, olives, pickles, and applesauce. We see more cans of fruit, vegetables, soups, stews, and milk. There are bottles of juice, water, salad dressing, cooking oil, and vinegar. And we see all kinds of cleaning supplies for the house, the laundry, and dishes.

Next we peek into a back room that is filled with boxes. These hold additional food and supplies to be used in emergencies such as floods, tornadoes, earthquakes, and ice storms. The food pantry helps many people. In God's world, it's important to share food with those who are hungry.

PRAYING:

Begin by reading today's Bible verse. Then **say: In this Bible verse, a hungry traveler is saved by eating figs and raisins given to him by kind people. In our world today, food pantries care for people by giving them the food they need to survive.** Have the children close their eyes and bow their heads for prayer.

EXPLORING:

Play the Mystery Fruit Bowl Game. Before Children's Church, gather fruit the children will be able to recognize by touch such as a banana, orange, apple, grapes, lemon, and pear. Place the fruit in a bowl and cover it with a cloth.

Begin the game by having the children stand in a circle. Hold up the Mystery Fruit Bowl. Explain that they will each get a turn to put their hands under the cloth and try to figure out what fruits are in the Mystery Fruit Bowl.

Go from child to child, asking them to keep their discoveries a secret. When every child has had a turn, ask everyone to call out the mystery fruits. Take the cloth off the bowl and reveal the mysterious contents.

GARDENS

SNACKING:

Serve a fruit snack such as fruit cocktail cups, individual boxes of raisins, or slices of fresh fruit.

SINGING:

"Climb, Climb Up Sunshine Mountain"; "Praise the Lord, All Creation."

MORE EXPLORING:

Children will enjoy coloring a **Care to Share Poster** that will serve as a reminder for people to donate to the local food pantry. Before Children's Church print: "Care to Share?" across the top of a sheet of posterboard. At the bottom print: "Give to our local food pantry." (You may want to include the actual name and a few more details specific to your church or community.) In the middle of the poster-board, draw large outlines of various fruits for the children to color.

When the children have finished decorating the poster, compliment them on their work. Explain that the **Care to Share Poster** will be posted at church, a local grocery store, or another location to remind people to share food with the hungry.

BIBLE VERSE:

"We remember . . . the cucumbers, the melons, the leeks, the onions, and the garlic; but now our strength is dried up."

(Numbers 11:5-6)

GARDENS

REMEMBERING VEGETABLES

MESSAGE:

Vegetables give us strength.

TWIRLING:

Ask the children to stand. Choose a child to spin the globe as you lead the children in **saying: Twirl and twirl God's wonderful world! Celebrate in Children's Church!** Next, ask everyone to twirl around once, then sit down.

SHARING:

Ask: If you were a super hero, and you ate a certain vegetable to make you strong, which vegetable would it be? *(Carrots. Corn on the Cob. Broccoli.)*

EXPLORING:

Lead the children in the Veggie Cheer. You will say each line of the cheer, then pause for them to repeat after you. Create a bit of rhythm by clapping.

Cheer: Peas, peas! (Pause.)

    We eat peas (Pause.)

    To be strong! (Pause.)

    We'll eat peas our whole life long! (Pause.)

    Beans, beans! (Pause.)

    We eat beans (Pause.)

    To be strong! (Pause.)

    We'll eat beans our whole life long! (Pause.)

Continue the Veggie Cheer, using some or all of these veggies: squash, tomatoes, onions, potatoes, corn, peppers, cabbage, cucumbers, okra, spinach, lettuce, broccoli, celery, and carrots. Finish the cheer by **exclaiming: We love God's gift of vegetables! Vegetables give us strength!**

PRAYING:

Show the children how to make "muscle man arms." Ask them to hold their arms this way as you pray.

42

EXPLORING:

To make Veggie Collages, you will need women's and/or cooking magazines, glue, scissors, and paper. Children will glue magazine pictures of vegetables onto a collage. Before Children's Church, go through the magazines and tear out pictures of vegetables and foods that feature vegetables. You will need several vegetable pictures per child.

Being by reading the Bible verse. **Say: The Hebrew slaves who followed Moses out of Egypt said these words as they walked through the wilderness. They really missed eating fresh vegetables, and they believed that they were losing their strength. God created vegetables to be colorful, tasty, and full of vitamins to give us strength!**

Give each child a sheet of paper. Explain that they are to trim around several vegetable pictures, then glue them to the paper. Suggest that their Veggie Collages will make wonderful refrigerator art!

SNACKING:

Serve a vegetable platter of carrots, cucumbers, and celery sticks, along with dip.

SINGING:

"God Made Me"; "Praise the Lord, All Creation."

MORE EXPLORING:

Children will enjoy creating "Vegetables for the Table" using play clay. Purchase play clay or use the following recipe to make your own.

To make Play Clay, in a saucepan mix two cups flour, one cup salt, and four teaspoons cream of tartar. To one cup water, add two Tablespoons of cooking oil and several drops of food coloring. Add the wet ingredients to the saucepan and stir. Cook over medium heat until the mixture begins to pull away from the sides of the pan and forms a ball. Cool, then knead. Store in an airtight container. This recipe should yield enough modeling dough for about ten children.

Give each child some clay. Demonstrate how to form specific vegetable shapes such as a round pea, a ruffled lettuce leaf, a lumpy potato, and a plump tomato.

PRAY:

God of Our World,
we are glad for all the vegetables in your great garden, especially our favorite ones. We want to be strong and healthy.
Amen.

BIBLE VERSE:

"THE FLOWERS APPEAR ON THE EARTH; THE TIME OF SINGING HAS COME, AND THE VOICE OF THE TURTLEDOVE IS HEARD IN OUR LAND."

(Song of Solomon 2:12)

FLOWERS APPEAR

MESSAGE:

Flowers are a sign of spring.

TWIRLING:

Ask the children to stand. Choose a child to spin the globe as you lead the children in **saying: Twirl and twirl God's wonderful world! Celebrate in Children's Church!** Next, ask everyone to twirl around once, then sit down.

SHARING:

Ask: What kind of flower do you like the best? *(Rose. Daisy. Daffodil.)*

LISTENING:

If practical, invite a gardener to visit Children's Church to answer some questions about flowers, gardens, and the seasons. Encourage your visitor to bring along any visual aids such as flowers, garden tools, or photographs of his or her garden. If you can't locate a gardener to visit, you may pose as the gardener and bring along some props such as a hat, gloves, and/or seed packets. Direct the following questions to the guest gardener or to yourself as the gardener.

Ask: When do flowers usually begin to appear? *(Springtime.)*

What makes the flowers, grass, and other plants turn green and bloom? *(More hours of sunlight and warmer weather.)*

How do flowers grow? *(Some sprout from seeds; some from a bulb in the ground; and others from bushes, stems, or vines that have been resting during the colder weather.)*

Why did God create flowers? *(Flowers feed birds, bees, and other creatures, including people, from pollen, nectar, seeds, or the fruit that grows from the flower. And of course, flowers are beautiful, too.)*

What do flowers need in order to grow? *(The right amount of sunlight, water, and food from the soil.)*

What kinds of flowers are a sign of spring where we live?

Encourage the children to ask a few questions of their own. Thank your guest or take off your gloves or hat to signal the end of Listening.

PRAYING:

Encourage the children to turn their faces into flowers! Have them lift their faces upward as if to the sun, then open their hands near the sides of their heads to create flower petals. **Pray.**

EXPLORING:

To make Filter Flowers, you will need cone-shaped coffee filters, crayons, a stapler, and chenille stems.

Begin by giving each child a coffee filter. Direct the children to color the outside of their filters. As the children finish, turn the filters inside out. This will be the inside of the flower. Next give them each a second filter to color. Once again, have them color the outside of the filters. (They may use a different color crayon.) This will be the outside of the flower.

To assemble the flower, place the first filter inside the second filter. Pinch together the base, then staple. Attach a chenille stem by twisting one end around the stapled base. Have the children hold up their creations in a flower show of spring flowers!

SNACKING:

Serve a snack of shelled and roasted sunflower seeds. These flower seeds are tasty, crunchy, and healthy. In the grocery store, sunflower seeds can sometimes be found with salad fixings and almost always where the nuts are displayed. Consider bringing in a picture of a sunflower to show to the children.

SINGING:

"My God Is So Great"; "Praise the Lord, All Creation."

MORE EXPLORING:

Sing and act out another version of the old standard, "This Is the Way." Lead the singing and the actions as the children follow along.

Sing: This is the way to hoe the ground (raise arms up and down as if

hoeing), **hoe the ground, hoe the ground.**

This is the way to hoe the ground, in God's wonderful garden.

This is the way to plant the seeds (wiggle fingers over floor) ...

This is the way to water the seeds (make a fist, point thumb to floor) ...

This is the way the seeds spring up (crouch down, jump up) ...

This is the way the leaves shoot out (extend arms in a v-shape) ...

This is the way the flowers bloom (cup upturned faces with hands, then open hands)....

PRAY:

God of Our World,
you created all
the seasons;
and there is
something
wonderful about
each one.
Today we
celebrate the
flowers that are a
sign of spring.
Amen.

45

"the tree grew great and strong, its top reached to heaven, and it was visible to the ends of the whole earth."

(Daniel 4:11)

GARDENS

46

GREAT TREES

MESSAGE:

God's creatures need trees.

TWIRLING:

Ask the children to stand. Choose a child to spin the globe as you lead the children in **saying: Twirl and twirl God's wonderful world! Celebrate in Children's Church!** Next, ask everyone to twirl around once, then sit down.

SHARING:

Ask: Do you have a favorite tree that you like to visit? *(The tree with a swing in it. The orange tree where I can pick my own oranges. The willow tree in the park that is a good place to play.)*

LISTENING:

Provide each child with a sheet of paper and crayons as you guide them in drawing Daniel's tree dream. It's from Daniel 4:10-12.

Say: **Today you're going to draw the Bible story as I read it to you.**

Read: **"Upon my bed this is what I saw; there was a tree at the center of the earth, and its height was great."**

Say: **Draw a tree trunk. Leave plenty of space at the top of your paper for the rest of the tree.** (Pause.)

Read: **"The tree grew great and strong, its top reached to heaven, and it was visible to the ends of the whole earth."**

Say: **Draw branches that stretch from the top of the tree trunk and reach high into the sky.** (Pause.)

Read: **"Its foliage was beautiful, its fruit abundant."**

Say: **Make beautiful leaves all over the tree branches.** (Pause.) **Color in lots of fruit among the leaves.** (Pause.) **"And it provided food for all. The animals of the field found shade under it."**

Say: **Draw animals under the tree.** (Pause.)

Read: **"The birds of the air nested in its branches."**

Say: **Add birds to your tree branches.** (Pause.)

Read: **"And from it all living beings were fed."**

Say: Draw a person under your tree. (Pause.) **Daniel's dream tree sounds wonderful. As I look around at your trees, I see that they are great and strong trees too!**

PRAYING:

Have the children stand in a circle, holding their pictures in front of them for everyone to see. **Pray.**

EXPLORING:

Brainstorm a big list of "Why We Need Trees" with the children, using a marker board or blackboard or a large sheet of paper. Make three categories: "Food from Trees," "Products from Wood," and "Other Good Uses." Here are some hints:

Food from Trees: Think of fruits from apples and bananas to oranges and pears, and nuts from almonds and beech to pecan and walnut. And don't forget maple syrup!

Wood Products: Consider all sorts of lumber and building materials used to make big things such as houses, furniture, boats, and pianos, and little things such as rulers, picture frames, and toothpicks.

Other Uses: List other ways that trees help God's world. These include oxygen and shade, medicine obtained from trees, homes for birds, bugs, and other creatures, and playful pursuits such as a place for swings and tree houses.

Make long lists, then count up reasons why we need trees!

SNACKING:

Serve applesauce topped with cinnamon, which is made from the inner bark of a tree, and/or maple syrup, which is made from the sap of a tree. Before children eat the snack, **sing or say the old camp song, "The Johnny Appleseed Grace": "Oh the Lord's been good to me, and so I thank the Lord, for giving me, the things I need: the sun, the rain, and the appleseed. The Lord's been good to me."**

SINGING:

"My God Is So Great"; "Praise the Lord, All Creation."

MORE EXPLORING:

Let the children enjoy some Christmas tree talk. **Ask: Does your family use a live tree with a root ball for replanting, a tree cut from the woods, a tree purchased from a Christmas tree lot, or an artificial tree? What is your favorite ornament on the tree? What kind of lights does your family use? When do you put up your tree?**

PRAY:

God of Our World, we are thankful for the beautiful, great, strong trees that you have created. Thank you for trees that give so much to animals, birds, and people. Amen.

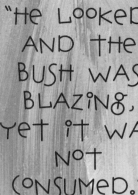

BiBLe VeRSe:

"He Looked, aND tHe BUSH WAS BLaZiNg, YeT iT WAS NoT CoNSUMeD."

(Exodus 3:2)

GARDENS

48

THE BURNING BUSH

MESSAGE:

God knows each of us by name.

TWIRLING:

Ask the children to stand. Choose a child to spin the globe as you lead the children in **saying: Twirl and twirl God's wonderful world! Celebrate in Children's Church!** Next, ask everyone to twirl around once, then sit down.

SHARING:

Ask: Can you tell us your fist name and last name? *(Miguel Carlos Sanchez. Elizabeth Anne Chin. Tiffany Nicole Marzetti.)*

LISTENING:

Share the story of God calling Moses by name.

Say: Once upon a time, there was a man named Moses who had a very interesting life. When he was a baby, his mother saved his life by putting him in a basket in the river. Then the Pharaoh's daughter found him and treated him as her own son. After living like Egyptian royalty, Moses began to worry about his fellow Hebrews, who were living as slaves in Egypt. Moses got into trouble helping one of these slaves, so he ran away.

Not long after, he married a shepherd's daughter. Moses became a shepherd, too. One day when Moses was leading the flock of sheep to new pastures, he saw a strange sight. There, on the side of Mt. Horeb, was a bush that was on fire, but not burning up. Moses decided that he had better have a closer look at the burning bush. When he did, the voice of God called to him from the bush, "Moses, Moses." Moses answered God saying, "Here I am." Then God told Moses that he must return to Egypt to save the Hebrew slaves. Moses, the man God called by name from the burning bush, still had a long and interesting life ahead of him!

PRAYING:

Invite the children to raise their hands when they hear their name called in the prayer. **Pray.**

EXPLORING:

Play the Roll Call Game using a sheet of paper for each child and a crayon or marker for printing names. Before Children's Church or on the spot, print the name of each child in large letters on a separate sheet of paper.

Just before the game, place the sheets of paper on the floor, as widely spaced as possible. To play the game, call upon the children by name, one by one, to find their name, stand on the paper, and shout, "Here I am!" When all of the names have been called, have the children hold up their papers and take turns declaring their names. **Say: God knows each of your wonderful names!**

Scramble the location of the names and play again, as time permits.

SNACKING:

Before Children's Church, place a drink box and an individually wrapped snack into a paper lunch bag, one for each child. **Say this rhyme each time as you hand out the snack bags: I'm so glad that you came! Come get your snack when I call your name!** (Call child's name.)

SINGING:

"The Lord Is My Shepherd"; "Be Still and Know."

MORE EXPLORING:

Let the children enjoy hearing their names as they play Call Ball. Locate or purchase a beach ball or other plastic ball. If practical, use a permanent marker to write every child's name on the ball.

Gather the children into a circle. Explain that you will call a child's name, then toss (or roll) the ball to that child. That child will catch the ball, then call another child's name, and toss (or roll) the ball to that child. Guide the game so that everyone's name is called. If time permits, have children switch places in the circle and play some more.

PRAY:

God of Our World,
we are happy that you
know each of us by
name:
(say each child's
name,)
and that you surround
us with your love.
Amen.

"one of them went out into the field to gather herbs."

(2 Kings 4:39)

GARDENS

50

HAPPY HERBS

MESSAGE:

God gave us flavors.

TWIRLING:

Ask the children to stand. Choose a child to spin the globe as you lead the children in **saying: Twirl and twirl God's wonderful world! Celebrate in Children's Church!** Next, ask everyone to twirl around once, then sit down.

SHARING:

Ask: What is your favorite flavor? *(Chocolate. Vanilla. Peppermint.)*

LISTENING:

Children will enjoy smelling the herbs and pretending to eat a meal at the Happy Herb House Restaurant. You will need either dry or fresh herbs and small bowls. (Look for fresh herbs in the produce section of the grocery store or from a local garden.) Find the following: chives or green onion tops; dill; rosemary or sage; parsley; basil, cilantro, or oregano; chervil, thyme, or savory; and mint. Put each of the seven needed herbs in separate bowls.

Gather the children into a circle. Tell them that when an herb is mentioned in the story, you will pass the bowl containing that herb. As the bowl is passed, they are welcome to touch and rub the herb as they smell it.

Say: Hooray! We're on our way to eat at the Happy Herb House Restaurant in beautiful Herbville. Look! The whole town is planted with pretty herb gardens. The herbs smell so nice and have such wonderful flavors.

Oh! Here's our restaurant. Let's go in now. The cooking smells make me feel even hungrier. The waitress wants us to sit down at this table. She's passing around thick slices of chive bread. (Pass the chives or onion tops.) **And she is bringing out bowls of dill pickles.** (Pass the dill.)

Here comes the rosemary (or sage) **pasta.** (Pass the rosemary or sage.) **Next she is bringing out the parsley potatoes.** (Pass the parsley.) **Now she's carrying out the basil** (or cilantro or oregano) **stewed tomatoes.** (Pass the basil, cilantro, or oregano.) **And here are the fresh peas seasoned with chervil** (or thyme or savory.) (Pass the chervil, thyme, or savory.)

Ah! What a delicious meal. Good thing we have room for some desert! It's mint chocolate chip ice cream pie. (Pass the mint.) I'm glad God gave us wonderful flavors.

PRAYING:

Give each child a sprig of herb to smell during the prayer.

EXPLORING:

For planting herbs, you will need paper or peat cups, potting soil, a bowl or bucket, scoop, water can or cup with water, and herb seeds. Dill and cilantro (grown from coriander seed) germinate readily. Before Children's Church, put the potting soil into the bowl or bucket, along with the scoop.

Have the children hold their cups over the bowl or bucket as you scoop in the soil. Next, put a pinch of the seeds into each child's palm. Have them press the seeds onto the top of the soil. Lightly moisten the soil in each cup to hold the soil and seed together.

Tell the children that at home, they are to place their cups on a saucer or plate, then put them on a window sill. They need to water their seeds a little in the morning and check to see if seeds need a bit more water in the evening. When the plants sprout, the whole cup may be placed in the garden or in a pot with more soil.

SNACKING:

Serve mint chocolate cookies or ice cream for a delicious snack!

SINGING:

"My God Is So Great"; "Shout to the Lord."

MORE EXPLORING:

Play the Silly Dilly Game. Invite the children to do the actions in the rhyme until they hear the word, "dill," then they must freeze in place until you begin again.

Say: Hop and pop as much as you will, (Pause.)

But you must stop when I say "Dill!" (Pause.)

Twist and turn as much as you will, (Pause.)

But you must stop when I say, "Dill!" (Pause.)

Wiggle and jiggle as much as you will, (Pause.)

But you must stop when I say, "Dill!" (Pause.)

Flutter and flop as much as you will, (Pause.)

But you must stop when I say, "Dill!" (Pause.)

PRAY:

God of Our World, thank you for filling your world with flavors! Amen.

51

BIBLE VERSE:

"I AM THE VINE, YOU ARE THE BRANCHES."

(John 15:5)

GARDENS

VINE OF JESUS

MESSAGE:

Christians are connected to one another through Jesus.

TWIRLING:

Ask the children to stand. Choose a child to spin the globe as you lead the children in **saying: Twirl and twirl God's wonderful world! Celebrate in Children's Church!** Next, ask everyone to twirl around once, then sit down.

SHARING:

Ask: Can you name a person you met or became friends with at church? *(I met Kirsten in the nursery when I was a baby. Mr. Bean, our organist is my friend. I met Tyler and Jamie just this year.)*

LISTENING:

Tell this story about children who are connected with one another through their church.

Say: Kisha carried a box into the fellowship room.

"What's in your box, Kisha," asked Nick.

"Triple chocolate brownies!" she said. "What's in your bag?" Nick answered, "My mom's famous fried chicken. I can't wait for this big supper to begin!"

The twins, Jonathan and David, pointed to a macaroni casserole on the table and said, "We helped make that!"

"Great," said Maria, "it's my favorite. Hey Kisha! My mom wants us to set out the napkins."

"Sure, I'll help," Kisha told her.

Nick's dad brought in an armful of decorations, and the boys hurried to help place them around the room. Then Kisha saw a boy and a girl she didn't know. She ran over and said, "Hi. My name is Kisha."

The new girl said, "We're Aaron and Kate. We're visiting."

Maria called out, "Come sit with us!" Soon the whole room was filled with good food and friendly people. The pastor rang the dinner bell and told them, "Jesus says, 'I am the vine, you are the branches.' We are here, we are all friends, and we are all Christians because we believe in Jesus." Next the

pastor said grace, thanking God for the food. Everyone said, "Amen!" Then all of the kids and all the grownups ate the delicious food as they enjoyed wonderful conversation and fellowship with their friends in Jesus Christ.

PRAYING:

Ask the children to hold hands or link pinkies. **Pray.**

EXPLORING:

Play the Vine Line Game!

Ask: **Has anyone seen a vine growing on a fence or trellis, reaching up a chimney or tree, or covering a wall?**

Say: **A vine can reach and climb and run a long way and it can have lots and lots of branches. Jesus is like a long, strong vine and all of us who believe in him are the branches. Let's play the Vine Line Game!**

Select a child to be the Vine. Have the child stand with feet slightly apart for balance, and arms raised at sides. Announce that the rest of the children will be the Branches. Explain that the Vine will *say: I am the Vine, you are the branches,* then call someone's name. The new Branch will come forward and reach out with one arm to touch the Vine. The Vine will repeat the verse, then call another name. The next Branch will come forward and touch the Vine. The Vine will continue to call out names until all the players are in the Vine Line. Play as time permits, letting other children take the part of the Vine.

SNACKING:

In celebration, serve small bunches of washed, seedless grapes.

SINGING:

"Jesus Loves Me"; "Shine, Jesus, Shine."

MORE EXPLORING:

For the Nice Bunch Poster, you will need a large sheet of paper or posterboard, purple or green paper, scissors, crayons, and glue. Before Children's Church, cut circles, one for each child. (Depending on how many children you have and how large your poster will be, you can determine the size of the grapes.)

Give the children each a circle, explaining that they are now holding a grape. Have the children draw their own faces onto the grape. When they are finished, glue the grape faces in a cluster onto the poster. With a crayon, draw a supporting vine and print the words, "A Nice Bunch!" You may want to write the name of each child next to her or his grape face. Hang the Nice Bunch Poster for all to admire.

PRAY:

God of Our World, we give you thanks for your Son, Jesus, and for all the people who believe in him. Amen.

people
in God's World

BiBLE VERSE:

"AND SHE GAVE BIRTH TO HER FIRSTBORN SON AND WRAPPED HIM IN BANDS OF CLOTH AND LAID HIM IN A MANGER, BECAUSE THERE WAS NO PLACE FOR THEM IN THE INN."

(Luke 2:7)

LITTLE BABIES

MESSAGE:

Babies need love and care.

TWIRLING:

Ask the children to stand. Choose a child to spin the globe as you lead the children in **saying: Twirl and twirl God's wonderful world! Celebrate in Children's Church!** Next, ask everyone to twirl around once, then sit down.

SHARING:

Ask: Have you ever helped take care of a baby? *(I held my new cousin. I helped give my baby brother a bath. I pushed my neighbor's baby in the stroller.)*

LISTENING:

To introduce the story, wrap a baby doll in a baby blanket. Show the baby doll to the chidden.

Say: I brought a baby with me this morning! I've fed the baby and talked to the baby and given the baby a bath and played with the baby and changed the baby and finally, the baby is asleep. Babies need so much love and care! Let's listen to a verse in the Bible about a mother taking care of a baby. Read Luke 2:7.

Ask: What is the name of this baby? *(Jesus.)* **And what is the name of the baby's mother?** *(Mary.)*

Say: Mary loved Baby Jesus, and she took good care of him. God wants us to love and care for babies too.

54

PRAYING:

Show your children how to fold their arms together and pretend they are rocking a baby. Ask them to slowly rock their baby as you pray.

EXPLORING:

To make Baby Faces Puppets, you will need plain white paper plates, yarn, staplers, and crayons. Beforehand, make a puppet for each child by stapling two paper plates together. Leave an opening at the bottom for a hand and secure a few strands of yarn at the top to make a tuft of hair. Make a puppet for yourself, too. On your puppet, draw a happy face on one side and a sad face on the other.

Give each child a paper plate puppet. Show the children your puppet and have them create happy and sad faces on theirs. When the puppets are complete, lead the children through this story, telling them that when the baby is crying, they are to hold up the sad face; and when the baby is laughing, they are to hold up the happy face. Use your puppet to prompt them.

Say: Betty the Baby was having a fussy day. First she cried because she was wet. (Sad face.) But then you changed her diaper, and she started to laugh. (Happy face.) Then she cried because she was hungry for her Happy Os Cereal. (Sad face.) So you gave her a whole bowl full of Happy Os, and she smiled and smiled. (Happy face.) Then she started fussing because she kicked off her ducky booties. (Sad face.) So you put them back on again and made them say, "Quack, quack." She started to laugh and laugh. (Happy face.)

But then you began to look at a book. It was a really good book, and you wanted to see what happened. Betty got mad because you weren't paying attention to her and started to really yell. (Sad Face.) So you showed her the pictures, and she began to smile. (Happy face.) When the book was over, you gave her a clown rattle to play with, and she dropped it. Betty let out a loud howl. (Sad face.) So you picked it up and made the clown dance and sing a silly song. Betty laughed and laughed. (Happy face.)

Betty started to cry because she was very tired and needed a nap. (Sad face.) So you put her into her crib. Soon she fell asleep. She had a little smile on her face because she was dreaming a happy dream. (Happy face.) And you had a huge smile on your face because Betty the Baby was asleep, and you needed a break. Babies need love and care, and that's hard work!

PRAY:

God of Our World,
we pray for babies everywhere, for babies need love and care!
Amen.

SNACK:

Serve applesauce, a traditional baby food that big kids and grownups enjoy, too!

SINGING:

"He's Got the Whole World"; "Go, Tell It on the Mountain."

MORE EXPLORING:

To make a We Love Babies Collage, you will need women's and parenting magazines, scissors, posterboard or craft paper, and glue. If your group is large, you may want to make more than one collage.

Before Children's Church, look through the magazines for pictures of babies and toddlers. Tear the pictures out, then trim around them.

Explain to the children that since babies love to look at photographs of other babies, your group will create a We Love Babies Collage for the church nursery. Have the children work together to fill the posterboard or craft paper with pictures. Remind them that in a collage, it's okay if the pictures overlap one another. Add a label that says, "We Love Babies!" Give the collage to someone on your church nursery staff, suggesting that it be hung where the babies can see it.

BIG KIDS

MESSAGE:

We ask questions as we grow.

TWIRLING:

Ask the children to stand. Choose a child to spin the globe as you lead the children in **saying: Twirl and twirl God's wonderful world! Celebrate in Children's Church!** Next, ask everyone to twirl around once, then sit down.

SHARING:

Ask: What do you look forward to doing when you are a bigger kid? *(I want to play Recreation Baseball. I'm going to be a cheerleader. I want to ride the school bus.)*

LISTENING:

As a cue card, make a large question mark on a sheet of paper. Hold up the question mark. **Ask: What's this?**

Say: This is a question mark. Every time a reader sees a question mark at the end of a sentence, it means that sentence is a question. I'm going to tell you a story about Jesus when he was a bigger kid. Every time I hold up the question mark, you are to *ask: "What happened next?"* **Practice this a few times, then begin.**

Say: In the Bible, we read about Jesus as a baby, and then we don't hear about Jesus again until he is a bigger kid. When Jesus was twelve years old, he went with his parents, Mary and Joseph, to a festival in Jerusalem. (Hold up question mark.) **When the festival was over, they started to return home, but Jesus stayed in Jerusalem.** (Hold up question mark.) **His parents thought he was with the other travelers in their group. They didn't realize that Jesus was missing until the end of a day's journey.** (Hold up question mark.) **They looked for Jesus among their relatives and friends but did not find him.** (Hold up question mark.) **They went back to Jerusalem to look for him.** (Hold up question mark.) **They looked for him for three days and finally found him in the Temple. Jesus was sitting among the teachers there, listening to them and asking questions.** (Hold up question mark.) **All who heard him were amazed at his understanding.** (Hold up question mark.) **Jesus went home with his parents. Jesus increased in wisdom as he grew. Asking questions helps all of us to increase in wisdom.**

BIBLE VERSE:

"AND WHEN HE WAS TWELVE YEARS OLD, THEY WENT UP AS USUAL FOR THE FESTIVAL."

(Luke 2:42)

PRAY:

Dear God, why do we ask questions as we grow? (Pause.) Because there's so much about God's world we want to know! (Pause.) Thank you, God. (Pause.) Amen. (Pause.)

PRAYING:

Have the children say each line of the prayer after you.

EXPLORING:

Plan on having one, two, or three bigger kids from your congregation come to Children's Church. Invite these bigger kids to share a skill they have such as playing a musical instrument, drawing, dancing, cheerleading, juggling, or speaking another language. Explain that they will demonstrate their skills for the children, then the children will be encouraged to ask questions.

Introduce your visitors by asking them a few general questions such as their names, ages, and where they go to school. Then ask them to demonstrate their skills.

When they are finished, guide your children in asking questions. For example, "Why did you decide to play the flute?" "How did you come up with that cartoon character?" or "Where do you take dance?" When the questions are finished, thank your visitors.

SNACKING:

Serve a snack enjoyed by kids of all ages, popcorn.

SINGING:

"Jesus Loves Me"; "O, How He Loves You and Me."

MORE EXPLORING:

Your children will love having the bigger kids join them in some fun games and activities. Consider a game such as Twister, floor puzzles, and/or marble runs and building sets.

PEOPLE

GOOD FRIENDS

MESSAGE:

Friends love one another.

TWIRLING:

Ask the children to stand. Choose a child to spin the globe as you lead the children in **saying: Twirl and twirl God's wonderful world! Celebrate in Children's Church!** Next, ask everyone to twirl around once, then sit down.

SHARING:

Ask: What is something nice a friend has done for you?
(Carlos shared his baseball glove with me. Shamika invited me to her birthday party. Foster let me ride his bike.)

LISTENING:

Begin by giving the children a thumbs up sign. **Say: Thumbs up to all of you! You are my friends, and I'm glad you are here. Friendship is a wonderful part of God's world. Here is a verse from the Bible that talks of friendship.** Read the Bible verse. **God wants us to be a good friend to others. As you listen to this story, make a thumbs up sign when you hear someone being a good friend. When you hear someone being a bad friend, make a thumbs down sign.**

Say: The kids were crowded onto the playground. Brandon was in a hurry to get down the slide so he pushed Liam. (Thumbs down.) **Sarah was mad that Brooke was using the sand sieve. She threw a handful of sand in Brooke's face.** (Thumbs down.) **Underneath the pine trees, Lizzie invited Laura to help her build a pine needle fort.** (Thumbs up.) **At the top of the jungle gym, Matt sang "Happy Birthday" to Martha, who was now seven.** (Thumbs up.)

At the bottom of the jungle gym, Jeb tripped Katherine as she was coming down the ladder. (Thumbs down.) **Merideth told Cliff that she thought his new shoes looked cool.** (Thumbs up.) **Just for fun, Adam threw a rock really hard at Tyrone.** (Thumbs down.) **Ricky was on crutches since he had a broken leg. When the whistle blew that recess was over, Ammar waited for Ricky and walked into school with him.** (Thumbs up.)

BIBLE VERSE: "A FRIEND LOVES AT ALL TIMES." (Proverbs 17:17)

God of Our
World,
friends love at all
times.
Help us to be
very good friends.
Amen.

PRAY:

Ask the children to form a circle. Send a handshake around the circle with the words, "I'm glad you're my Children's Church friend." Next ask children to link elbows. **Pray.**

EXPLORING:

To make Friendship Sticks, you will need craft sticks (the size of tongue depressors), gummed stars, markers, tape, and ribbon or yarn in two colors. Precut ribbon or yarn into two-foot lengths, one of each color for each child.

Explain to the children that in some Native American tribes, it was the custom to present a friendship stick as a sign of friendship and peace. Tell the children that they are each going to make a Friendship Stick to present to a special friend.

Have each child write her or his own name down one side of the stick. Then have the children turn their sticks over and write the name of a friend down the other side. (You may need to assist with the name writing.) Next invite them to put gummed stars around the names. Finally, help the children tie each color of ribbon to the bottom of the stick, securing with a knot on one side and tape on the other. Explain that they are to give the Friendship Stick to the friend whose name is on it.

SNACKING:

Explain to children that friends share with one other. Have the children form pairs. Serve them a snack that comes in a single serving package such as pretzels or crackers. Give a package to each pair and invite them to enjoy sharing with one another.

SINGING:

"I Love to Take a Walk"; "Hine Ma Tou (How Good and Pleasant.)"

MORE EXPLORING:

Children will love ringing the Friendship Gong in honor of their friends. A pot lid and large metal spoon make an excellent gong. Invite the children to come forward one at a time and *say: I'm ringing the Friendship Gong for my friend (friend's name.)* If time permits, go another round or two.

people

OLDER PEOPLE

MESSAGE:

Older people share their wisdom with us.

TWIRLING:

Ask the children to stand. Choose a child to spin the globe as you lead the children in **saying: Twirl and twirl God's wonderful world! Celebrate in Children's Church!** Next, ask everyone to twirl around once, then sit down.

SHARING:

Ask: What is the name of someone you know who is old? *(Mrs. Perkins. My great grandma. The man who lives next door.)*

LISTENING:

Tell the children that you are going to slowly begin to count. When they hear their age, they are to stand up. Begin counting until all of the children are standing.

Say: I didn't need to count very long! That's because, even though you are growing up and having birthdays every year, you aren't very old yet. (Invite the children to sit down for the rest of the story.) **There is a man in the Bible named Methuselah who was very, very old.** (Say the name again and ask the children to repeat it with you several times.) **Methuselah was the grandfather of Noah. He lived to be nine hundred and sixty-nine years old. If we played our stand up game with Methuselah, we would have to count for a very long time before Methuselah stood up!**

In God's world, many people live long lives. We gain wisdom as we live. When you live a long life and grow to be old, you learn many things. At church, in our families, and our neighborhoods, it's good to listen to the wisdom of older people.

PRAYING:

Ask the children to bow their heads for the prayer.

EXPLORING:

Invite an older member of your congregation to visit with the children and share some wisdom. Remind your guest that the children are young and may have a limited attention span, but they will love to hear lively stories and anecdotes. Encourage your guest to bring along any visual aids such as photographs, awards, or souvenirs.

BIBLE VERSE:

"THUS ALL THE DAYS OF METHUSELAH WERE NINE HUNDRED SIXTY-NINE YEARS."

(Genesis 5:27)

PRAY:

God of Our World, thank you for all the years of our lives. Thank you for older people who have lived many years and have lots of wisdom to share with us. Amen.

Begin by introducing your guest to the children. After the guest has finished speaking, invite the children to ask questions.

SNACKING:

Light birthday candles on a cake, pan of brownies, pie, or other snack. Have the children *sing: Happy Birthday to you. Happy Birthday to you. Happy Birthday everyone in God's world. Happy Birthday to you.* Serve your guest the first piece!

SINGING:

"He's Got the Whole World"; "Come Bless the Lord."

MORE EXPLORING:

Children love to talk about their own grandparents. Guide the conversation by **asking specific questions: Can you tell us the name of your grandparents? Do you know how old they are? Where do they live? What do you like to do best with them? Can you remember something wise they have told you?**

MY PARENTS

MESSAGE:

God wants us to listen to our parents.

TWIRLING:

Ask the children to stand. Choose a child to spin the globe as you lead the children in **saying: Twirl and twirl God's wonderful world! Celebrate in Children's Church!** Next, ask everyone to twirl around once, then sit down.

SHARING:

Ask: What is the name of your mother and your father? *(Judy and Martin. Miguel and Sofia. Jackson and Sherry.)* As you talk about parents, be sensitive to children who may not know both of their parents, children whose parents are divorced or deceased, and children who are living in foster situations.

LISTENING:

If practical, bring in a photograph of your own mother and/or father.

Say: There is a book in the Bible called the "Book of Proverbs." Proverbs is a collection of wise sayings. Listen to one of those wise sayings. Read Proverbs 1: 8-9. **This means that the things your parents teach you will help you as you grow up. Parents love you and want you to live happy, good, and safe lives. God wants you to listen to your parents.**

If you have brought in a photo of your parents, show it to the children now, then tell them something your mother and/or father taught you. Next, ask the children to close their eyes and picture their own mother and father. Have them open their eyes again and one at a time, tell the group something their mother and/or father has taught them.

Conclude by **saying: Parents, and the things they teach us, are part of God's plan for the world. Parents are a very good idea!**

PRAYING:

Ask the children to picture their parents as you pray.

EXPLORING:

To make Loving Lockets, you will need dessert or luncheon size paper plates, crayons, hole punch or stapler, and ribbon or yarn.

BIBLE VERSE:

"FOR THEY ARE A FAIR GARLAND FOR YOUR HEAD, AND PENDANTS FOR YOUR NECK."

(Proverbs 1:9)

PRAY:

God of Our World, thanks for moms and dads, and the things they teach us. Help us to be good listeners. Amen.

Give each child two paper plates. **Say: A locket is a necklace with pictures of loved ones. Today you're going to make Loving Lockets to wear home to surprise your parents.**

Have the children color the faces of their mothers on one plate and their fathers on another. (Those children in non-traditional situations may draw other caregivers or relatives.) Staple the plates locket-style, with the pictures on the inside, along the left side to create a hinge. To make hangers, staple a length of ribbon or yarn about twenty-four inches long to the top of one of the plates. Knot the ribbon or yarn at the top so the children can wear the lockets.

Explain to the children that they are to wear their lockets home. Once at home, they can find a place to hang them up as decorations in honor of their parents.

SNACKING:

Play Silly Manners as children eat their snacks. **Say: Parents teach their children table manners. Just for fun, today we're going to eat our snacks using silly manners.**

Serve a simple snack that uses a spoon, such as applesauce or pudding, and serve drinks in paper cups with straws. **Give silly instructions such as: Before you take a bite, see if you can balance your spoon on your head, Let's hear you slurp!** and **Who can blow the loudest bubbles with their straws?**

SINGING:

"He's Got the Whole World"; "Come, Bless the Lord."

MORE EXPLORING:

Lead the children in a few rounds of Mother May I? Have them line up on one side of the room. One at a time, give them each instructions to move forward. They may only move if they *say: Mother may I?* first. If they forget to *say: Mother may I?* they must go back to the starting place. **Use fun instructions such as: Jenny, you may hop three steps forward because you brushed your teeth as I told you to** or **Jackson, you may take a twirling step forward because you listened when I said, "No more cookies!"** The game is over when all of the children have crossed the room.

MANY TEACHERS

MESSAGE:

We have many teachers who help us learn.

TWIRLING:

Ask the children to stand. Choose a child to spin the globe as you lead the children in **saying: Twirl and twirl God's wonderful world! Celebrate in Children's Church!** Next, ask everyone to twirl around once, then sit down.

SHARING:

Ask: What is the name of one of your teachers? *(Ms. Workman. Mr. Chin. Mrs. Brizendine.)*

LISTENING:

The following story takes children on a pretend walk around town to see the many teachers at work.

Say: Teachers are important people in God's world. There are verses in the Bible that speak of teachers. Here's one of them. Read the Bible verse. We have many teachers who help us learn. Some of those teachers are at school, but we have teachers in other places, too. Listen to this story that takes a pretend walk around a town to see all of the teachers.

First, here is the Happy Hands Preschool. Ms. Pink is teaching the children the colors of the color wheel: red, orange, yellow . . . . But now we're walking past the Delightful Days Daycare. Ms. Weeks is teaching the children the days of the week. Monday, Tuesday, Wednesday . . . .

Now we're at the Skip to My Lou Elementary School. In the kindergarten room, Mr. Melody is teaching the children to sing: There was a farmer had a dog, and Bingo was his name . . . . But let's peek into a first grade class. Mrs. Seven is teaching the children to add: one plus one is two, two plus two is four, four plus four is eight . . . . But look at the fifth graders! Ms. Microscope is demonstrating a science experiment. In ten seconds, a volcano is going to erupt. Ten, nine, eight . . . .

There's the school bell! School is out, but teachers are still teaching. At the Tippy Toes Dance Academy, Madame Pirouette is teaching the students their ballet positions: first position, second position, third position . . . . And on the T-Ball Field, Coach Batterup is showing the kids the proper way to swing a bat: Keep your eyes on the ball . . . .

BIBLE VERSE:

"I WILL INSTRUCT YOU AND TEACH YOU THE WAY YOU SHOULD GO."

(Psalm 32:8)

God of Our World, thank you for the many teachers who help us learn. We thank you especially for the teacher whose face we see right now. (Pause.) Amen.

Look into the church window. Pastor Church is planning out his children's sermon for Sunday: "Good morning boys and girls . . . ." And look, Mrs. Craft has just arrived with a handful of supplies for her Sunday school lesson on Sunday: glitter glue, feathers, and play clay . . . . And finally, let's peek into one of the houses in the neighborhood. Jason's mother is showing him how to tie his shoes: loop like bunny ears . . . . and Claire's father is teaching her how to juggle: one orange, two orange, three oranges . . . . There are teachers everywhere!

PRAYING:

Ask the children to picture the face of one of their teachers as they listen to the prayer.

EXPLORING:

To make Teacher Folders, you will need folders and precut letters, numbers, and/or shapes stickers. If you can't find these stickers, provide other colorful stickers. Explain to the children that teachers have a lot of papers, so a pretty folder is a perfect present. Have the children use the stickers to decorate a folder for their favorite teachers.

SNACKING:

Explain that years ago, it was the custom to bring an apple to the teacher. That's why apples have become a symbol for teachers. Serve a delicious snack of apple slices with a dip made of one cup plain yogurt, one half cup brown sugar, and a dash of cinnamon.

SINGING:

"He's Got the Whole World"; "Bless the Lord."

MORE EXPLORING:

Lead the children through an action game showing ways they can help their teachers: sharpening pencils, picking up blocks, cleaning the board, feeding the fish, sweeping the classroom, and washing the cafeteria table. Encourage the children to come up with other ways to help teachers, too.

people

OUR PASTOR

MESSAGE:

The pastor leads our church.

TWIRLING:

Ask the children to stand. Choose a child to spin the globe as you lead the children in **saying: Twirl and twirl God's wonderful world! Celebrate in Children's Church!** Next, ask everyone to twirl around once, then sit down.

SHARING:

Ask: What is something you like about our pastor? *(He makes really good baked beans. Pastor Augustine tells fun children's sermons. Our pastor can kick the ball really far in kickball.)*

LISTENING:

Explain to your pastor that you will be talking in Children's Church about the role of the pastor, with this message: "The pastor leads our church." Ask the pastor to write the children a simple letter explaining some of the ways that he or she leads your church. Pastors are busy, so give yours plenty of notice! If it's not possible to get a letter from the pastor, you can simply list some of the ways your pastor leads the church.

Begin by saying a few words about your pastor and reinforcing some of the comments the children made during Sharing. Then **say: The word "pastor" comes from the Latin word for "shepherd." The pastor leads our church just as a shepherd leads his sheep. Sometimes, the people in a pastor's congregation are called his or her "flock." That's us! As a surprise today, I have a letter written to you by our pastor.**

Read the letter. Conclude by **saying: To thank our pastor for the letter, we're going to send a surprise back. In just a few minutes, we're going to make a poster for our pastor.**

PRAYING:

Invite the children to huddle together as a flock. **Pray.**

EXPLORING:

To make a Pastor's Flock Poster, you will need posterboard, cotton balls, glue, and crayons. Before Children's Church, print at the top of the posterboard: "Love to you from your flock." Estimate how many children you have, and draw the simple outline of a sheep (oval body, triangular head with oval ears, and stick legs) for each

BIBLE VERSE:

"The gifts He gave were that some would be apostles, some prophets, some evangelists, some pastors and teachers." (Ephesians 4:11)

PRAY:

God of Our World, thank you for sending our pastor (pastor's name) to lead our flock. Amen.

67

child. Add a few extra sheep in case you have more children than expected. If your group is large, make two posters. Green posterboard will work well, since the green can be the field for the sheep. If you have white posterboard, consider having the children draw green grass around their sheep.

Bring out the posterboard and read the greeting to the children.

Say: And you're each going to be one of the sheep on the poster! Have the children glue cotton balls to the body of a sheep, then sign their names next to the sheep. When the poster is finished, admire it and lead the children in a chorus of "Baa" in honor of the lovely, puffy flock. Perhaps the children can help you deliver the poster as soon as possible.

SNACKING:

Check with your pastor ahead of time to determine one of his or her favorite snack foods. **Explain to the children: We're having grapes because Pastor Coyle just loves grapes!** Have the children help you pack up some of the snack to leave for the pastor as a treat.

SINGING:

"He's Got the Whole World"; "Come, Bless the Lord."

MORE EXPLORING:

Play the Lead the Flock Game. Explain to the children that you are the shepherd, and they are the flock. Encourage them to "Baa" in their loudest voices during the game. Have them follow you as you lead them in hopping over a fence, splashing through a steam, squeezing through a gate, hiding from a hungry wolf, and grazing in a green pasture. If time permits, let the children take turns as the shepherd.

SYMBOLS in God's World

BOAT AFLOAT

MESSAGE:

The boat is a symbol of the church.

TWIRLING:

Ask the children to stand. Choose a child to spin the globe as you lead the children in **saying: Twirl and twirl God's wonderful world! Celebrate in Children's Church!** Next, ask everyone to twirl around once, then sit down.

SHARING:

Ask: Have you ever taken a boat ride? *(When we went with my neighbor on the lake. I went in a canoe at camp. We took the ferry last summer.)*

LISTENING:

Read children the story of the Calming of the Storm.

Say: There is a story about a really scary boat ride in the Bible. The people riding in the boat were Jesus and his disciples. Listen: (Read the story of Jesus calming the storm from Mark 4:35-41.)

Ask: Were the disciples scared? *(Yes.)* **What was Jesus doing during the storm?** *(Sleeping.)* **When the disciples woke him up, what did Jesus say to the storm?** *("Be still!")* **What happened to the storm?** *(The wind ceased, and the sea was calm.)* **Were the disciples impressed that even the wind and the sea obeyed Jesus?** *(Yes.)*

BIBLE VERSE:

"A GREAT WINDSTORM AROSE, AND THE WAVES BEAT INTO THE BOAT, SO THAT THE BOAT WAS ALREADY BEING SWAMPED."

(Mark 4:37)

Thanks, God,
for boats that
float,
a symbol of our
church.
Thank you, God,
for sailing with
us.
A-a-a-a-men.

SYMBOLS

70

Say: **This story helped the disciples understand that Jesus could perform miracles such as calming a scary storm that was rocking a boat. The boat, or ship, is now a symbol of the church. We, the people of the church, sail on the boat. God watches over the boat as we sail in calm times and scary times, too.**

PRAYING:

Teach the children this prayer to the tune of "Row, Row, Row Your Boat."

EXPLORING:

To make Stormy Ship Pictures, you will need colored chalk, white paper, and bowls of water. When dampened, chalk forms bolder lines; and the colors become more vibrant.

Demonstrate how to dip the chalk into the water before each chalk stroke. Encourage the children to use the sides of the chalk, too as they create swirling waters, stormy skies, and colorful sails.

SNACKING:

Serve individual cups of blue gelatin. While not necessary, clear plastic glasses makes the blue sea look more inviting. Encourage children to use spoons to turn their calm gelatin seas into stormy ones! Tell them that this sea tastes lots better than real sea water!

SINGING:

"Peace Like a River"; "I Have Decided to Follow Jesus."

MORE EXPLORING:

Share some other seaworthy Bible stories with the children such as the story of Noah and the Flood or Jonah and the Great Fish. Your church or local library may have picture books of these stories that the children will especially enjoy.

FOOT ON GOD'S PATH

MESSAGE:

Christians walk in the path of God.

TWIRLING:

Ask the children to stand. Choose a child to spin the globe as you lead the children in **saying: Twirl and twirl God's wonderful world! Celebrate in Children's Church!** Next, ask everyone to twirl around once, then sit down.

SHARING:

Ask: Have you ever walked on a path? *(The path that leads through my grandma's garden. I walked on a path at the park.)*

LISTENING:

Let the children use their feet in this active story.

Say: Christians walk in the path of God. Listen to a Bible verse that talks about walking in God's path. Read the Bible verse. **Say: Let's play a story game to help us think about walking in God's paths. First we need to warm up.** Ask the children to stand. Lead them in *saying: Step, step, step, step* as they walk in place. Tell them that they will do this after every line of the story.

When we listen carefully in Sunday school and Children's Church, we walk in God's path. *(Step, step, step, step.)*

When we pray, we walk in God's path. *(Step, step, step, step.)*

When we worship during the church service, we walk in God's path. *(Step, step, step, step.)*

When we bring in cans for the food pantry, we walk in God's path. *(Step, step, step, step.)*

When we send a card to someone who is sick, we walk in God's path. *(Step, step, step, step.)*

When we welcome new kids to our church, we walk in God's path. *(Step, step, step, step.)*

When we share and when we say we are sorry, we walk in God's path. *(Step, step, step, step.)*

When we follow the Ten Commandments and teachings of Jesus, we walk in God's path. *(Step, step, step, step.)*

BIBLE VERSE:

"MY STEPS HAVE HELD FAST TO YOUR PATHS; MY FEET HAVE NOT SLIPPED."

(Psalm 17:5)

PRAY:

Step, step, step, step.
God please help us follow your path.
Step, step, step, step.
Amen.

When we try our best to live as the Bible tells us to live, we walk in God's path. *(Step, step, step, step.)*

PRAYING:

Explain to the children that the foot is a symbol of those who follow God's path. Ask the children to walk in place as you pray.

EXPLORING:

Before Children's Church, use yarn to mark out a winding path. If practical, create the path outdoors. If not, wind the path down a hall-way and into other rooms. If you can't do this, create a path in the space you have, perhaps in a spiraling fashion. Place the snack in a basket or backpack at the end of the path.

Read the Bible verse to the children again. **Say: Let's follow the yarn path! Try to step carefully, with one foot in front of the other. Stay on the path and do your best not to let your feet slip.** Lead the children in walking the path slowly. When they dis-cover the snack at the end, explain that people who walk along paths are often on a hike or picnic.

SNACKING:

Pack a simple snack into a basket or backpack. When the children discover the snack, you may have them eat it at that location or bring it back to the usual place where the snack is served each week.

SINGING:

"Praise the Lord Together"; "I Have Decided to Follow Jesus."

MORE EXPLORING:

Show children how to play Follow the Leader on the yarn path. You can be the first leader and have them follow you as you do silly walks, twirls, backward steps, hops, and skips. Next, let other chil-dren take turns as the leader.

BOOK OF THE WORD

MESSAGE:

The Bible is the word of God.

TWIRLING:

Ask the children to stand. Choose a child to spin the globe as you lead the children in **saying: Twirl and twirl God's wonderful world! Celebrate in Children's Church!** Next, ask everyone to twirl around once, then sit down.

SHARING:

Ask: What is the title of one of your favorite books? *(Where the Wild Things Are. My Big Bible Storybook. Goodnight Moon.)*

LISTENING:

The following verses talk of the importance of the Bible. Lead the children in saying each verse along with you after you read it.

Say: The Bible is a very important book for Christians. The Bible contains the word of God. These words help us know how God wants us to live. Listen as I say each Bible verse, then we'll say it together.

Isaiah 40:8: "The grass withers, the flower fades; but the word of our God will stand forever."

Proverbs 3:1: "My child, do not forget my teaching, but let your heart keep my commandments."

John 1:1: "In the beginning was the Word, and the Word was with God, and the Word was God."

Isaiah 34:16: "Seek and read from the book of the Lord."

Say: As you grow and become better and better readers, you can read the word of God yourself in the Bible!

PRAYING:

Have the children hold out their hands to resemble an open book. **Say: An open book is a symbol of the Bible.** Next ask the children to close their hands and fold them for prayer.

BIBLE VERSE:

"Seek and read from the book of the Lord."

(Isaiah 34:16)

PRAY:

God of Our World,
help us to open our Bibles again and again as we read your word.
Amen.

EXPLORING:

Play Bible Word Roll with a ball or another object that can be rolled. Have the children sit or stand in a circle. Roll the ball to a child **saying:** (child's name,) and **The Bible word is** (fill in a Bible word.) That child will roll the ball back to you *saying: The Bible word is (and say the Bible word.)*

Here is a list of Bible words to use in the game: Love, God, Jesus, commandment, Holy Spirit, scroll, faith, follow, listen, shepherd, world, stars, boat, cross, dove, fish, bread, light, heaven, disciples, angels, gifts, pray, manger, heart. To extend the game, open the Bible and find more words to call out.

SNACKING:

Serve the children fruit roll ups. (You may want to cut each fruit roll up in half.) **Say: These are pretend scrolls. In Bible times, the Bible was written on long rolls called "scrolls."**

SINGING

"The B-I-B-L-E"; "Everywhere I Go."

MORE EXPLORING:

Invite someone in your congregation to be your special guest reader. Ask your guest to read the children a Bible story. Consider presenting your guest and your children ribbons or bookmarks for their Bibles.

SYMBOLS

THE CHRISTIAN CROSS

MESSAGE:

Christians are proud of the cross.

TWIRLING:

Ask the children to stand. Choose a child to spin the globe as you lead the children in **saying: Twirl and twirl God's wonderful world! Celebrate in Children's Church!** Next, ask everyone to twirl around once, then sit down.

Ask: What is something that make you proud? *(My mother is a really good cook. I can tie my shoes. I learned to swim across the pool.)*

LISTENING:

Make a cross out of paper. Use the cross to cue the children during the story.

Ask: What's this? *(A cross.)*

Say: The cross is the most important Christian symbol. Christians are proud of the cross! Jesus died on the cross, but he rose from the dead on Easter Sunday. Because of this, the cross became a happy and important symbol of our faith. I'm going to tell you a story about a girl named Maria who is proud of the cross. To help me tell the story, every time I hold up my paper cross, you are to shout together: *Cross.*

One Sunday morning, Maria woke up and spotted the *(cross)* **she had made in Sunday school hanging from her mirror. After she put on her church clothes, she remembered the** *(cross)* **necklace her grandma had given her. She slipped the** *(cross)* **over her neck. At breakfast she noticed that her mom was wearing a** *(cross)* **too and her dad had on his** *(cross)* **tie tack.**

As she walked toward her church she saw the *(cross)* **on top of the steeple and the** *(cross)* **on the church sign.**

When she got to Sunday school, she noticed the *(cross)* **on the welcome poster on the door and the wooden** *(cross)* **on the table.**

The first thing she noticed when she stepped into the church for worship was the *(cross)* **over the altar. When the pastor came in, Maria noticed that she was wearing a** *(cross)* **on her robe. Then she looked at the church bulletin and saw a**

"MAY I NEVER BOAST OF ANYTHING EXCEPT THE CROSS OF OUR LORD JESUS CHRIST."

(Galatians 6:14)

75

PRAY:

God of Our
World,
we are
Christians,
and we are
proud of the
cross!
Amen.

(cross) **and at the hymnal and saw a** (cross) **there too. Crosses were everywhere! Maria felt proud to see so many crosses and she felt proud to be a Christian.**

PRAYING:

Have children cross their arms in front of them to form a cross. **Pray.**

EXPLORING:

Make a Giant Cross of Crosses! You will need paper and crayons.

Give the children each two or three sheets of paper and crayons. Ask them to fill their sheets with lots of crosses. Next, call the children forward one at a time to help you lay out a giant cross. When the cross is laid out, have everyone walk along the edges of the cross. After a few minutes, ask the children to hold their arms high in the air and *say: We are proud of the cross!*

If you have a place to display it, consider taping together the Giant Cross of Crosses and placing it somewhere in your church for all to admire.

SNACKING:

Lead the children in saying or singing the nursery rhyme, "Hot Cross Buns":

Hot cross buns, hot cross buns,

One a penny, two a penny, hot cross buns.

Serve rolls or biscuits and invite the children to decorate them with a cross of frosting.

SINGING:

"Jesus"; "Living Christ, Bring Us Love."

MORE EXPLORING:

Make People Crosses! Line your children up to form a cross. When everyone is in place, have them hold their hands high in the air and *shout: We are proud of the cross!* Let the children take turns directing the formation of more People Crosses.

ROCK LIKE OUR GOD

MESSAGE:

God is forever.

TWIRLING:

Ask the children to stand. Choose a child to spin the globe as you lead the children in **saying: Twirl and twirl God's wonderful world! Celebrate in Children's Church!** Next, ask everyone to twirl around once, then sit down.

SHARING:

Ask: Can you tell us about a rock you have seen or found? *(I collected pebbles at the beach and put them in a jar. My neighbor brought me a rock from Mexico. I saw lots of pretty rocks at the Science Museum.)*

LISTENING:

You will need a good sized rock, but one that's not too heavy for the children to hold.

Begin by holding up the rock. **Ask: What's this? Say: You're right! This is a rock. Ask: If I jumped on the rock, would it break?** *(No.)* **If I spilled hot water on the rock, would it melt away?** *(No.)* **If I put the rock in the washing machine, would it crumble?** *(No.)* **If I left it out in the rain, would it shrivel up?** *(No.)* **If I tossed the rock into the fireplace, would it burn up?** *(No.)*

Say: Rocks last for a long, long time. Because of this, the symbol of the rock is used to help us understand that God is forever. Listen to what Hannah said in her prayer to God. Read the Bible verse, then pick up the rock. **Say: In honor of the symbol of the rock, I'm going to call you forward, one at a time. When it's your turn, hold the rock and** *say: My name is _____, and God is my rock.*

PRAYING:

Ask the children to make a fist with one hand. **Say: Pretend your fist is a rock. Rest it in the palm of your other hand while we pray.**

EXPLORING:

Before Children's Church, cut out seven stepping stones from construction paper. Tape the stepping stones to the floor, a few feet apart so that the children can jump from stone to stone.

Say the Bible verse again. Explain to the children that they will take turns jumping from stepping stone to stepping stone as everyone *calls out the verse: There is no rock like our God.* Ask the children to pretend that the stones are set into a rushing river. If time permits, have the children jump the stones again, this time moving in the opposite direction.

SNACKING:

Serve Rocky Road Pudding. Invite the children to stir mini-marshmallows, raisins, or another kind of candy into vanilla pudding or yogurt.

SINGING:

"Walking With Jesus"; "Living Christ, Bring Us Love."

MORE EXPLORING:

To play "Rock, Rock, Whose Got the Rock?" you will need a rock that can easily be passed from child to child. Have the children stand or sit in a circle, close to one another. Choose a child to stand in the middle of the circle. Explain that the children will pass a rock behind their backs, being careful not to let the child in the circle see who has the rock at any given time. (Children who aren't passing the rock can pretend to be passing it to add to the confusion.) After the rock has passed around the circle for a few minutes, **call out: Rock, rock, whose got the rock?** and have the child in the center take a guess. The child who has the rock will then take a turn in the center.

HELPING HANDS

MESSAGE:

We use our hands to help others.

TWIRLING:

Ask the children to stand. Choose a child to spin the globe as you lead the children in **saying: Twirl and twirl God's wonderful world! Celebrate in Children's Church!** Next, ask everyone to twirl around once, then sit down.

SHARING:

Ask: What is a way you helped someone else this week? *(I called up my Grandma to say "hello." I tied my cousin's shoe for her. I helped my teacher put away the crayons.)*

LISTENING:

Place the following items into a bag: a pen, a whisk, a spatula or other cooking utensil, a sponge or scrub brush, a book, a toy animal, and a tool such as a hammer or wrench.

Say: We use our hands everyday in God's world. One of the best ways to use our hands is to help others. Listen to this Bible verse about a woman who uses her hands to help. Read the Bible verse.

Hold up the bag. **Say: In this bag, I have some items to get us thinking about ways we can use our hands to help others.** Pull out each item, one at a time. Let the children tell ways that item can be used to help others. Here are some ideas:

Pen: We can write cards and letters to cheer up people who are sick or lonely.

Cooking Utensil: We can cook a meal for someone who is hungry or who has just moved into our neighborhood.

Sponge or Scrub Brush: We can help an elderly person clean his or her house, or we can help our parents when they are tired.

Book: We can read to someone who is feeling sad, or we can lend the book to someone who is sick in bed.

Toy Animal: We can use the animal to entertain a baby who is crying, or we can give it to a shelter for homeless children.

Tool: We can use the tool to fix a house that has been damaged in a hurricane, or we can help make repairs at our church.

Say: There are so many ways we can use our hands to help others!

BIBLE VERSE:

"SHE OPENS HER HAND TO THE POOR, AND REACHES OUT HER HANDS TO THE NEEDY."

(Proverbs 31:20)

PRAY:
God of Our
World,
thank you for
helping hands.
Amen.

SYMBOLS

80

PRAYING:

Have the children form a circle, then join hands. Explain that you are going to send a prayer squeeze around the circle. You will squeeze the hand of the child on your right, who will then squeeze the hand of the child on his or her right. This will continue until the squeeze has gone all the way around the circle. Invite the children to bow their heads and close their eyes. Start the squeeze. When the squeeze has come back to you, begin the prayer.

EXPLORING:

To make Fancy Hands Greetings, you will need white paper, crayons, and decorative stickers such as stars and/or hearts.

Explain to the children that they are going to make Fancy Hands Greetings to send to someone in your church who needs a bit of extra love. (You may want to give the name of the person or persons. Consider newcomers, the elderly, shut-ins, and those who are sick.)

Have the children use one hand to trace the outline of the other hand onto the paper. Have them write "Love *(name)*" somewhere on the page, outside of the hand. Then invite the children to use crayons and stickers to decorate the hand.

Mail or deliver the Fancy Hands Greetings as soon as possible.

SNACKING:

Let the children help you make Helping Hands Delight. You will need an angel food, sponge, or pound cake; one can of fruit cocktail; one package of pudding, mixed; one container of whipped topping; mixing and serving bowls; and spoons.

First, have all of the children wash and dry their hands, **saying: Cooking hands are clean hands.** Let them take turns breaking the cake into pieces into the bottom of the serving bowl, then spooning in the pudding, the fruit cocktail, and the whipped topping. Serve the Helping Hands Delight by dipping down through the layers.

SINGING:

"Praise the Lord Together"; "Walk With Me (Chorus only)."

MORE EXPLORING:

Play the Helping Hands Glove Challenge. Let the children choose partners. Set out a pair of stretch gloves. Have the children take turns putting a glove on their partner's hands. When both partners are wearing a glove, have them do high fives as everyone *shouts out: Hooray for Helping Hands.*

PLACES
in God's World

BIG SKY

MESSAGE:
God's skies have all kinds of weather.

TWIRLING:
Ask the children to stand. Choose a child to spin the globe as you lead the children in **saying: Twirl and twirl God's wonderful world! Celebrate in Children's Church!** Next, ask everyone to twirl around once, then sit down.

SHARING:
Ask: What is your favorite type of weather? *(I like big snowstorms. Sunshine, but with white puffy clouds. I like rainy days.)*

LISTENING:
Today's story is set at Camp Big Sky!

Say: Let's pretend we are at Camp Big Sky in the foothills of the Goofy Mountains. We are sitting around a cozy campfire tasting marshmallows and listening to our camp leader and local weatherman, Sunny Storm.

Sunny says, "While you're camping at Camp Big Sky, we want you to see the sky at night: twinkling with millions of stars, glowing in the moonlight, and dusted with meteor showers. During the day, we want you to watch the sky to learn about the weather. God created the sky and all the weather the skies hold.

BIBLE VERSE:

"HE ANSWERED THEM, 'WHEN IT IS EVENING, YOU SAY, 'IT WILL BE FAIR WEATHER, FOR THE SKY IS RED.'"

(Matthew 16:2)

PRAY:

God of Our World, we praise you for the night sky and the day sky and for all of the world's weather. Amen.

82

When I was just a boy, I came to Camp Big Sky. The week I stayed here, it was warm and sunny, then cooler and partly cloudy, then cool and cloudy, then cold and rainy, then rainy and very windy, then there was a snow flurry, and on the last day, it was warm and sunny again. The weather was exciting!

This week I think there is a good chance that we'll see a red sky, some gray clouds, a rainbow, a blue sky, and some white clouds. At Camp Big Sky, we keep our eyes to the skies! OK, Campers, say it with me, 'At Camp Big Sky, we keep our eyes to the skies!'" (Ask the children to repeat with you.)

PRAYING:

If practical, have the children look up at the sky through a window or door as you pray. If not, ask them to picture the sky in their favorite type of weather.

EXPLORING:

To create Weather Skyscapes, you will need markers, glue, cotton balls, white paper, and a small bowl of water. Bring out the supplies in stages.

Begin by asking the children to use markers to color their favorite type of weather, from a snowstorm to clouds and rain to rainbows and blue, sunny skies. Next, bring out the cotton balls. Invite the children to glue them to their pictures to add snow and/or fluffy clouds. (Cotton balls can be unrolled to create longer smoother effects if desired.) Finally, offer a wet but not dripping cotton ball to any child who wants to add a watery touch to the sky. A light swabbing will give a slight blur to raindrops or soften a rainbow.

Admire the finished pictures, commenting that you're sure that Sunny Storm would like them too!

SNACKING:

Create Fair Weather Fluff! Set blue gelatin in a glass bowl or individual cups. Top with dollops of whipped cream clouds.

SINGING:

"Heavenly Sunshine"; "This Is the Day."

MORE EXPLORING:

Use a simple game to teach the children a weather proverb. Before Children's Church, cut out two clouds from pink or red paper, or color red clouds and cut them out. Behind one cloud, glue or tape a sun shape. Glue or tape a crescent moon on top of the other cloud.

Hold up the sun and cloud. **Say: Red sky in the morning, travelers take warning.** Have the children repeat this rhyme with you.

Hold up the moon and cloud. **Say: Red sky at night, travelers delight.** Have the children repeat this rhyme with you.

Tell the children that Jesus knew about these weather signs and that even in Bible days, people understood that a red sunset often meant good weather the next day. A red sky at sunrise often means stormy weather. Read Matthew 16:2-3. Let the children take turns holding up the clouds and as each is raised, lead them in the appropriate line of the weather rhyme.

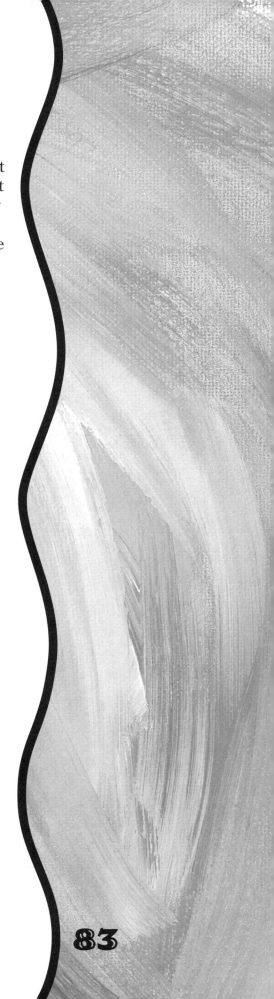

"JUST AFTER
DAYBReAK,
JeSUS STOOD
ON THe
BeACH;
BUT THe
DiSCiPLeS
DiD NOT
KNOW THAT
iT WAS
JeSUS."

(John 21:4)

JESUS AT THE SHORE

MESSAGE:

God's people gather on the shore.

TWIRLING:

Ask the children to stand. Choose a child to spin the globe as you lead the children in **saying: Twirl and twirl God's wonderful world! Celebrate in Children's Church!** Next, ask everyone to twirl around once, then sit down.

SHARING:

Ask: What is something fun to do at the shore? *(Make sand castles. Fly kites. Play catch.)*

LISTENING:

The following story is taken from John 21:4-14. Invite the children to repeat your hand motions.

Say: Just after daybreak, Jesus stood on the beach; (Wave.) **but the disciples did not know that it was Jesus. Jesus said to them,** (Cup hands around mouth.) **"Children, you have no fish, have you?" They answered him, "No."** (Make a zero with thumb and forefinger.) **He said to them, "Cast the net to the right side of the boat,** (Point right.) **and you will find some." So they cast it, and now they were not able to haul it in because there were so many fish.** (Make a fist and pull.) **The disciple whom Jesus loved said to Peter, "It is the Lord!"** (Tap palm against forehead.) **When Simon Peter heard that it was the Lord, he put on some clothes, for he was naked, and jumped into the sea.** (Pinch nostrils.) **But the other disciples came in the boat, dragging the net full of fish, for they were not far from the land,** (Point straight ahead.) **only about a hundred yards off.**

When they had gone ashore, they saw a charcoal fire there, with fish on it, and bread. (Rub tummy.) **Jesus said to them, "Bring some of the fish that you have just caught.** (Wiggle hand in a forward motion.) **So Simon Peter went aboard and hauled the net ashore,** (Make a fist and pull.) **full of large fish, a hundred fifty-three of them;** (Move fingers as if counting.) **and though there were so many, the net was not torn.** (Scratch head.) **Jesus said to them, "Come and have breakfast."** (Beckon with hand.) **Now none of the disciples dared to ask him, "Who are you?" because they knew it was the Lord. Jesus came and took the bread and gave it to them,** (Extend open palm outward.) **and did the same with the fish. This was**

now the third time (Hold up three fingers.) **that Jesus had appeared to the disciples after he was raised from the dead.**

PRAYING:

Have the children fold their hands for prayer.

EXPLORING:

To make Sandy Shore Snapshots, you will need fine or medium grade sandpaper (whole or half sheets) and crayons.

Say: Jesus gathered with his disciples at the seashore; but people also gather at the shores of lakes, rivers, bays, sounds, and even ponds. The shore is the place where the land meets a body of water.

Invite the children to imagine something fun they would like to do at the shore or a toy they would like to use at the shore. Have them draw a picture of the scene or the toy on the sandpaper. Encourage them to use bold colors and strokes as they fill in their picture.

When the Sandy Shore Snapshots are finished, have the children hold them up as they tell about their sandy shore fun.

SNACKING:

Make quick and easy Buried Treasure Buckets to delight your group! You'll need graham cracker crumbs, small candies, gummy fish, cups, and spoons. Layer the candy treasure into the bottom of the cup, then cover with graham cracker sand. When you serve the snack, invite the children to dig into their cup buckets with spoon shovels to find the treasure.

SINGING:

"He's Got the Whole World"; "This Is the Day."

MORE EXPLORING:

Play the Silly Shorebirds Game. Ask the children if they have ever seen the birds who scurry at the edge of the shore to avoid the lapping water. Let them pretend to be silly shorebirds as they try to get as close as they can to the imaginary water line. Wiggle a long length of ribbon or crepe paper streamer along the floor to create a fluctuating shoreline.

PRAY:

God of Our World, we like knowing that Jesus gathered with his disciples on the shore. Today, your believers still like to gather on the shore! Amen.

"WHeN THe LoRD DeSCeNDeD UPoN MoUNT SiNAi, To THe ToP oF THe MoUNTAiN, THe LoRD SUMMoNeD MoSeS To THe ToP oF THe MoUN-TAiN, AND MoSeS WeNT UP."

(Exodus 19:20)

86

MOSES ON THE MOUNTAIN

MeSSAge:

God gave us rules for living.

TWiRLiNg:

Ask the children to stand. Choose a child to spin the globe as you lead the children in **saying: Twirl and twirl God's wonderful world! Celebrate in Children's Church!** Next, ask everyone to twirl around once, then sit down.

SHARiNg:

Ask: What is a rule at your house? *(Brush your teeth twice a day. No running inside. Don't eat in the living room.)*

LiSTeNiNg:

Sing the story to the tune of "On Top of Old Smoky."

Sing: Up out of Egypt, the Hebrews had fled.
   They followed Moses and did what he said.

   Through the big wilderness, the people did roam.

   They kept on walking to find their new home.

   They came to a mountain, a holy place.

   They set up their camp at Mt. Sinai's base.

   Moses went up to speak to the Lord,

   And warned all the people not to explore.

   On top of Mount Sinai, all covered with smoke,

   The Lord God came down to talk to all of the folk.

   Through lightning and fire, God spoke like thunder,

   Filling the Hebrews with awesome wonder.

   Then God called up Moses and Aaron, too, and told them the ten rules that are right, strong, and true. We follow these Ten Commandments to this very day,

   As we go to school, to work, and to play.

Say: On top of Mount Sinai, Moses was given the Ten Commandments by God. The Ten Commandments are rules for living. God gave us rules to help us know the difference between right and wrong and to show us how to live.

PRAYING:

Have the children touch their fingertips together over their heads to resemble a mountaintop. **Pray.**

EXPLORING:

Generate a bit of excitement by making an old-fashioned volcano! To set up the volcano, place a teacup or other one cup container in a shallow bowl or pan. Mold some modeling dough or clay around the container to simulate a mountain shape. Into the container, place one Tablespoon of baking soda, layer on one Tablespoon of dish detergent, then add a few drops of food coloring. In a separate container, have one to two cups of vinegar at hand.

Say: The Bible describes Mount Sinai as crackling with lightning, booming with thunder, flashing with fire, covered in smoke, and shaking greatly. This sounds a lot like a volcano. Not all mountains are volcanoes and even those that are volcanoes are not active very often. Sometimes, when a volcano erupts, it has a flow of melted rock called "lava."

Bring out the pretend volcano. Pour about one third of a cup of vinegar to start. When the initial fizz begins to slow, add another measure of vinegar. The dregs of soap and soda can be reactivated several times by adding more vinegar.

SNACKING:

The children will have fun sculpting Potato Volcanoes. Before Children's Church, make mashed potatoes, cutting back slightly on the liquid to assure that the mixture is a bit stiff. You will also need shredded cheddar cheese.

Warm up the potatoes, if they have cooled. Give each child a dollop of potatoes on a plate, along with a spoon. Invite the children to use their spoons to shape the potatoes into a mountain with a volcanic hole in the center. Finish by spooning a bit of the cheese into each volcano.

SINGING:

"Climb, Climb Up Sunshine Mountain"; "Walk With Me."

MORE EXPLORING:

Children have definite opinions about rules! Give them some time to talk about house rules, school rules, good rules, and bad rules. Discuss why people make and follow rules. Have a Bible handy and refer to Exodus 20:2-17 to cross reference any of the rules mentioned by the children with the Ten Commandments.

PRAY:

God of Our World,
your world is a better place when people follow your rules.
Through the Ten Commandments,
we learn how to love you and love one another.
Amen.

MESSAGE:

We tell others about Jesus.

TWIRLING:

Ask the children to stand. Choose a child to spin the globe as you lead the children in **saying: Twirl and twirl God's wonderful world! Celebrate in Children's Church!** Next, ask everyone to twirl around once, then sit down.

SHARING:

Ask: Do you have any news? *(I got a kitten. My mom is sick. We're going to the zoo after church.)*

LISTENING:

Children will travel along with Paul to tell the good news of Jesus on Paul's first journey. Before Children's Church, make nine signposts for the following destinations: Seleucia, Salamis, Paphos, Attalia, Perga, Antioch, Iconium, Lystra, and Derbe. Tape the signposts to the floor in the order listed, spacing them as you wish. Have the children walk along with you as you tell the story.

Say: Paul, an early believer in Jesus, wanted to tell everyone the good news of Jesus Christ. In Bible days there were no telephones, televisions, daily newspapers, or internet. News was spread by travelers who told the news to those they met. Travelers also carried letters.

Let's travel with Paul on his very first trip to tell others about Jesus. Paul and his friend, Barnabas, got on a boat at Seleucia. (Step to signpost.)

From Seleucia they sailed to the island of Cyprus to the town of Salamis. (Step to signpost.) **Paul said, "Good news! Jesus is the Messiah God promised!"**

From Salamis they went through the island to the town of Paphos. (Step to signpost.) **Paul said, "Good news! Jesus is God's son!"**

Paul then sailed from the island to the mainland town of Attalia. (Step to signpost.) **Paul said, "Good news! Jesus worked miracles!" Paul traveled on to Perga.** (Step to signpost.) **Paul said, "Good news! Jesus healed people!"**

From Perga he went to Antioch. (Step to signpost.) Paul said, **"Good news! Jesus taught us how to live as we should!" Paul**

left Antioch and went to Iconium. (Step to signpost.) **Paul said, "Good news! Jesus came to save everyone!"**

From Iconium he went to Lystra. (Step to signpost.) **He said, "Good news! Jesus will forgive our sins!" After Lystra Paul went to Derbe.** (Step to signpost.) **He said, "Good news! Jesus promises life."**

Then Paul turned around, traveling (Follow signposts.) **from Derbe to Lystra to Iconium to Antioch to Perga to Attalia, telling others about Jesus. He and Barnabas sailed back to Seleucia.** (Step to signpost.)

PRAYING:

Ask the children to hold hands in one long chain. **Pray.**

EXPLORING:

Lead the children in the Island Hopping Game. Tape sheets of paper to the floor in a random fashion, one per person, including yourself. Invite everyone to stand on a paper island.

Say: An island is a piece of land that is surrounded on all sides by water. There are islands in rivers, lakes, and seas. We will now pretend we are standing on islands. I'll start the game by sailing over to one of you to whisper some good news. As soon as I tell you, I'll sail back to my island. You will sail off to another person to whisper the same good news, then sail home to your own island. We'll play until everyone has had a turn to sail and tell good news.

Begin by **whispering: Jesus loves you!** into one player's ear. Once the game is finished, begin another round or two of island hopping, as time permits.

SNACKING:

English muffin halves make great islands! Toast halves, then spread with cream cheese tinted green. For extra fun, let the children add sprinkles to represent people and animals.

SINGING:

"O, How I Love Jesus"; "This Is the Day."

MORE EXPLORING:

Write up the Children's Church Good News Newsletter. On a large sheet of paper or posterboard, print a bit of news that each child shares with you. Encourage parents to read over the news when they arrive for their children.

PRAY:

God of Our World, help us to tell others about Jesus just like Paul did. Amen.

BIBLE VERSE:

"YOU MAKE SPRINGS GUSH FORTH IN THE VALLEYS; THEY FLOW BETWEEN THE HILLS."

(Psalm 104:10)

90

IN THE VALLEYS

MESSAGE:

Living things need water.

TWIRLING:

Ask the children to stand. Choose a child to spin the globe as you lead the children in **saying: Twirl and twirl God's wonderful world! Celebrate in Children's Church!** Next, ask everyone to twirl around once, then sit down.

SHARING:

Ask: Do you have a favorite water activity? *(It's fun to ride in a boat. I like to go swimming at the pool. Running through the sprinkler is my favorite.)*

LISTENING:

To add sound effects to the story, fill an empty plastic bottle or other watertight container halfway with water. You will make sloshing sound effects with the water every time you mention a water activity in the story.

Say: Wallace Womble Waterford, also known as "Wally," woke up at eight o'clock. Wally went into the bathroom and after a minute, flushed the toilet. (slosh) Then Wally washed his hands (slosh) and his face. Wally walked downstairs and drank a glass of water (slosh) because he was thirsty. Wally thought the cat, whose name was "Wee Willie Winkie" might be thirsty too. Wally filled Wee Willie Winkie's bowl with water. (slosh)

Wally ate a big bowl of his favorite cereal, then rinsed out his bowl with water. (slosh) Next, he put on his bathing trunks and went outside to help his parents with some Saturday chores. His mom was already washing their dog, Woof, with shampoo and soon Wally rinsed Woof with the hose. (slosh) His dad was already soaping the car and before long was ready for Wally to turn the hose to the car. (slosh) Wally helped his mom water the garden (slosh) and his dad water a newly planted tree. (slosh) Wally noticed that the honeybees and butterflies were drinking the water (slosh) from little puddles in the soil. That made him remember to put water in the bird bath. (slosh)

It was getting hot outside and everyone had been working hard, so now Wally and his parents were thirsty. They went inside for tall glasses of water. (slosh) Wally's dad said wasn't it wonderful to live in a valley that had plenty of good water from the streams, a river, and a lake. Wally's mom said that the water from springs and from rain fill the streams, the river, and the lake. Wally replied that it's a good thing, because the plants, people, birds, bugs, and animals that live in the valley all need wonderful water.

PRAYING:

Invite each child to slosh the water bottle before you offer the prayer.

EXPLORING:

No matter how wonderful water is, some children still need to be enticed into the bathtub. To make Splashing Bath Salts, you will need baking soda, inexpensive cologne, essential oil, or vanilla extract, food coloring, and sandwich size zippered bags.

Ask the children to come to you one by one. Have them hold open a bag as you measure in four Tablespoons of baking soda. Add a few drops of the scent of your choice and a few drops of food coloring. Seal the bag, pressing out most of the air.

When all the bags are sealed, tell the children to gently squeeze, rub, and prod the contents of the bag to mix. Explain that Splashing Bath Salts are a treat for bath time. With the permission of a parent, they are to put the salts into their bath water to make bath time more fun.

SNACKING:

If it's in season, serve wonderful, water-filled watermelon. Find a seedless variety, if you can. Prepare by slicing the melon, then cutting the rind off of each slice. Dislodge any seeds with a fork. Cut the melon into bite-sized pieces and store in the refrigerator until it's time for Children's Church. If you can't locate watermelon, serve another snack made with water such as cool pops.

SINGING:

"He's Got the Whole World"; "Glory Be to God on High."

MORE EXPLORING:

Lead the children in singing a few water-inspired songs such as the "Eensy, Weensy Spider"; "Row, Row, Row Your Boat"; "Jack and Jill"; and "Peace Like a River."

PRAY:

God of Our World,
water is important in so many things we do.
Thank you for the water we use and enjoy every day.
Amen.

BIBLE VERSE:

"THEN THEY CAME TO ELIM, WHERE THERE WERE TWELVE SPRINGS OF WATER AND SEVENTY PALM TREES; AND THEY CAMPED THERE BY THE WATER."

(Exodus 15:27)

AT THE OASIS

MESSAGE:

God gives us what we need.

TWIRLING:

Ask the children to stand. Choose a child to spin the globe as you lead the children in **saying: Twirl and twirl God's wonderful world! Celebrate in Children's Church!** Next, ask everyone to twirl around once, then sit down.

SHARING:

Ask: Can you remember a time when you felt very hungry or very thirsty? *(I got very hungry on a car trip. I was really thirsty after playing T-Ball. When I wake up in the morning, I am hungry and thirsty.)*

LISTENING:

Use the storytelling standard "Going On a Bear Hunt" as your guide for leading children in "Going on an Oasis Hunt." Invite them to repeat each line after you and to join you in slapping thighs.

Say: Moses and the Israelites... (Slap thighs, right, left, right, left.)
    Were escaping Egypt...
    They didn't want to stay...
    So they had to go...
    Into the wilderness...

    The people were hungry...
    The people were thirsty...
    They didn't want a salty sea...
    They didn't want a dry desert...
    They wanted an oasis...

    Going on an Oasis Hunt!...
    Have to cross the Red Sea...
    Can't go over it...
    Can't go under it...
    Gotta' go through it...

    Going on an Oasis Hunt...
    Gotta walk along a valley...
    Can't go around it...
    Can't go between it...
    Gotta' go through it...
    Going on an Oasis Hunt...
    Look, there's the oasis!...

It has twelve springs...
It has seventy palm trees...
We're going to camp here!

Moses and the Israelites were hungry and thirsty from traveling such a long way. They depended on God to give them the things they needed to live in the wilderness. God gives us what we need, too.

PRAYING:

Ask the children to bow their heads. **Pray.**

EXPLORING:

Place a shoe, a jacket, a water bottle, a box or can of food, a Bible, a bed sheet, a photo or magazine picture of a family, and a photo or magazine picture of friends into a bag or pillowcase.

Say: We're going to use the items in this bag to help us talk about the things we need from God. As I hold up an item, you can take turns coming up with reasons why we need those things.

Here are some ideas:

Family Photo: Families love us, care for us, and help us.

Food Box or Can: Our bodies need food in order to live.

Sheet: Sheets are something we usually sleep on. People need sleep to be healthy.

Photos of Friends: Friends are people who share in our everyday lives. They play and talk and laugh and cry with us.

Shoe: Shoes protect our feet from hot and cold ground and from things that are sharp, squishy, stinging, or dirty.

Bottle of Water: Our bodies need water in order to live.

Bible: The Bible tells us about God, Jesus, our Christian faith, and how God wants us to live our lives.

Jacket: Jackets protect us from being too cold or getting a sunburn. People need clothes and coats to protect their skin.

SNACKING:

Children will have fun snacking in a pretend oasis. You will need a sheet or sheets to spread on the floor, a construction paper leaf for every child, small bottles or cups of water, and dried dates or another fruit, cut into bite-sized pieces.

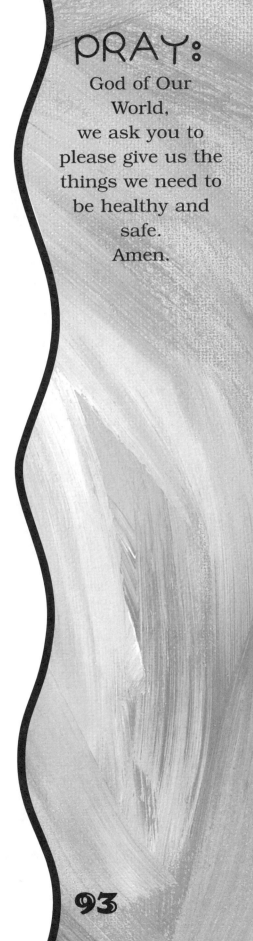

PRAY:

God of Our World,
we ask you to please give us the things we need to be healthy and safe.
Amen.

Invite the children to sit in the oasis you have created. Serve each child the water and a paper leaf with one or two dates or other fruit placed on top of it.

Say: **An oasis is usually a place in the dry, hot, sandy desert where there is water. And because there is water, plants and trees can grow in an oasis. A desert oasis gives water, shade, food, and rest. Moses was glad to find an oasis with twelve springs of water and seventy palm trees.**

SiNGiNG:

"He's Got the Whole World"; "Walk With Me."

MORE EXPLORING:

To make My Home Oasis Pictures, you will need paper and crayons.

Say: **Our pretend oasis gave us a spot where we could eat, drink, and rest. Your home is like an oasis too, because when you are home you have a place to eat, drink, rest, be with your family and friends, and talk about God.**

Invite the children to draw pictures of their homes or favorite spots in their homes such as comfortable chairs or beds of their own.

HAPPY FIELDS

MESSAGE:

Be happy in God's world.

TWIRLING:

Ask the children to stand. Choose a child to spin the globe as you lead the children in **saying: Twirl and twirl God's wonderful world! Celebrate in Children's Church!** Next, ask everyone to twirl around once, then sit down.

SHARING:

Ask: Can you tell us something that makes you happy? (*I love to open Christmas presents. Having my friends over to play. My new puppy makes me very happy.*)

LISTENING:

To tell this interactive story, divide the children into four groups: The Green Grass, The Wild Weeds, The Fragrant Flowers, and The Vegetable Vines. (You may want to color a symbol to place in front of each group.) Ask the children to listen for the name of their group as you tell the story. When they hear their group's name, they are to jump up, wave their arms, and *shout: We're happy!* Tell them to sit right down again after they shout. Practice this a few times, then begin.

Say: When the spring comes to God's great fields, the sun shines warmer and the gentle rain waters the ground. The seeds and roots of the plants wake up and begin to grow: The Green Grass (pause), **The Wild Weeds** (pause), **The Fragrant Flowers** (pause), **and The Vegetable Vines** (pause).

Summer comes to God's great fields. The Green Grass (pause) **grows thick. The Wild Weeds** (pause) **rise tall. The Fragrant Flowers** (pause) **begin to bloom. The Vegetable Vines** (pause) **send out shoots and leaves.**

The autumn of the year comes to God's great fields. The Green Grass (pause) **sways tall in the wind, showing off golden seed stalks. The Wild Weeds** (pause) **have become giants, covered with mighty stickers, cotton puff seeds, and strong stalks. The Fragrant Flowers** (pause) **are covered with bunches of colorful blossoms sending sweet smells into the air. And the Vegetable Vines** (pause) **are loaded with beautiful and tasty cucumbers, tomatoes, beans, pumpkins, grapes, and gourds.**

BIBLE VERSE:

"Let the field exult, and everything in it."

(Psalm 96:12)

95

PRAY:

God of our world,
we are happy to
be here!
Amen.

When winter comes to God's great fields, it is time for the **Green Grass** (pause), **The Wild Weeds** (pause), **The Fragrant Flowers** (pause), **and The Vegetable Vines** (pause) **to rest. All year long, God's fields are happy, and we are happy to be part of God's world, too!**

PRAYING:

Have the children stand and wave their arms during the prayer, as they did during the story. **Pray.**

EXPLORING:

There are so many happy activities to enjoy in a field! Lead the children in acting out riding horses, flying kites, catching lightning bugs and letting them go again, playing kickball, throwing sticks for dogs to fetch, tossing Frisbees™, picking flowers, eating grapes from a vine, and laying down in the soft grass to watch the clouds.

SNACKING:

Another happy activity to enjoy in a field is a picnic. Use a picnic hamper or cooler to hold the snack. Ask the children to imagine that they are sitting at a picnic table or spread a blanket on the floor. Create a little fun by pretending to brush away picnic ants, point to a beautiful cloud, or hold onto your paper napkin because it is so windy.

SINGING:

"Heavenly Sunshine"; "Glory Be to God on High."

MORE EXPLORING:

Children love to tell about their own happy experiences outside in God's world. Invite them to share memories of riding a tricycle or bicycle; playing on a playground; or going to a park to swim, hike, or picnic. Remember too, the activities the church may sponsor such as egg hunts, church picnics, and fellowship retreats.

NUMBERS
in God's World

ONE LORD

MESSAGE:
We are one in God.

TWIRLING:
Ask the children to stand. Choose a child to spin the globe as you lead the children in **saying: Twirl and twirl God's wonderful world! Celebrate in Children's Church!** Next, ask everyone to twirl around once, then sit down.

SHARING:
Ask: Can you name just one thing you know about God? *(God loves us. God made the world. God had a son named Jesus.)*

LISTENING:
Children will have fun celebrating the Number One in this action story.

Say: Let's have fun with the Number One. It's an important number, so we're going to play an action game that celebrates the Number One. Listen carefully!

Clap one time for the one Lord Jesus. (Pause.)

Stand up one time for our one faith in him. (Pause.)

Tap your head one time for the one baptism. (Pause.)

Hold up one finger for the one God. (Pause.)

Hug yourself one time because God loves each one of us. (Pause.)

Cross your arms one time for the one cross. (Pause.)

Wave your hands one time as one believer. (Pause.)

Bow your head one time for the one Lord's Prayer. (Pause.)

BIBLE VERSE:

"ONE LORD, ONE FAITH, ONE BAPTISM, ONE GOD AND FATHER OF ALL, WHO IS ABOVE ALL, THROUGH ALL AND IN ALL."

(Ephesians 4:5-6)

PRAY:

God of Our World,
we thank you for
the one faith that
we have in your
one Son, Jesus
Christ.
We praise you for
the one baptism,
the one Bible,
and the one
Christian Church.
Amen.

Place one hand over your heart for the one Bible. (Pause.)
Jump for joy one time because we are one in God! (Pause.)

Now, let's say our big list of Number One things. Repeat after me: One Lord Jesus. (Pause.) **One faith in him.** (Pause.) **One baptism.** (Pause.) **One God.** (Pause.) **God loves each one of us.** (Pause.) **One cross.** (Pause.) **I am one believer.** (Pause.) **One Lord's Prayer.** (Pause.) **One Bible.** (Pause.) **We are one in God.** (Pause.)

PRAYING:

Have children hold up one forefinger as the Number One. **Pray.**

EXPLORING:

To make Number One Bible Bookmarks, you will need construction paper, masking tape, scissors, and crayons. Before Children's Church, cut the paper into strips about two-and-one-half inches wide. Using the masking tape, put a large number "1" on each bookmark.

Give everyone a bookmark embellished with the number "1." Invite the children to make crayon rubbings around the tape. When they finish, help them peel off the tape to reveal a clean number "1" image. **Say: Use your Number One Bible Bookmark to mark your place in your Bible or Bible storybook to help you remember that we are one in God.**

SNACKING:

Offer the children a snack food that resembles the Number One such as a cool pop, a granola bar, or a string cheese stick. Point out that there is one snack for each one of them, shaped like the...what? Number One!

SINGING:

"His Banner Over Me Is Love"; "Children, Go Where I Send You."

MORE EXPLORING:

For the One Is Fun Hunt, you will need five or six types of small treasures such as stickers, bouncy balls, wrapped candy, fun adhesive bandages, and pretty pencils. Have one of each of these items per child. Hide the items before Children's Church.

Explain the rules of the hunt beforehand. **Say: In honor of the Number One, we'll have a One Is Fun Hunt. In this hunt, you are allowed to take only one of each type of treasure you find. When the hunt is over, everyone will have one of everything. Show kindness and help one another as you hunt, because we are one in God.**

TWO OF EVERY KIND

MESSAGE:

God's animals are amazing.

TWIRLING:

Ask the children to stand. Choose a child to spin the globe as you lead the children in **saying: Twirl and twirl God's wonderful world! Celebrate in Children's Church!** Next, ask everyone to twirl around once, then sit down.

SHARING:

Ask: Can you tell us which two of God's animals are your favorites? *(Dogs and cats. Horses and guinea pigs. Lions and tigers.)*

LISTENING:

Ask the children to participate in the story of Noah loading his ark by *saying: Two of every kind* after you name an animal.

Say: Listen to a very old story about a very old man who filled a very large boat with very many animals. The Lord

God told Noah that a very big rainstorm was coming. Soon a very deep flood would cover the earth. The Lord God told the very old Noah to build the ark. When it was finished the Lord God told Noah to load the very big boat with two animals of every kind. So Noah searched very far and very wide to find the very many animals.

These are the animals Noah loaded into the very big boat two by two: monkeys, (pause) cats, (pause) lions, (pause) chickens, (pause) giraffes, (pause) lizards, (pause) ostriches, (pause) gorillas, (pause) guinea pigs, (pause) bears, (pause) horses, (pause) mice, (pause) tigers, (pause) reindeer, (pause) foxes, (pause) goats, (pause) ducks, (pause) elks, (pause) opossums, (pause) dogs, (pause) rabbits, (pause) sheep, (pause) camels, (pause) llamas, (pause) snakes, (pause) antelopes (pause) elephants, (pause) turtles, (pause) kangaroos, (pause) birds, (pause) pigs, (pause) wolves, (pause) anteaters, (pause) moose, (pause) beaver, (pause) squirrels (pause) hamsters, (pause) deer, (pause) koala, (pause) alpaca, (pause) wildebeests, (pause) prairie dogs, (pause) raccoons, (pause) and yaks. (pause) Two of each kind of God's very amazing animals were saved on the ark!

BIBLE VERSE:

"AND OF EVERY LIVING THING, OF ALL FLESH, YOU SHALL BRING TWO OF EVERY KIND INTO THE ARK, TO KEEP THEM ALIVE WITH YOU; THEY SHALL BE MALE AND FEMALE."

(Genesis 6:19)

PRAY:

God of Our World,
we are very happy that you created so very many amazing animals.
We thank you and Noah very much for saving two of every kind.
Amen.

PRAYING:

Have the children bow their heads for prayer.

EXPLORING:

To make Two By Two Bracelets, you will need construction paper or card stock, a variety of animal stickers in duplicates, scissors, and tape. Before Children's Church, cut paper into strips wide enough to accommodate the animals stickers. Strips should be about seven inches long.

Give each child a bracelet strip. Spread out the stickers for the children to examine, keeping duplicates together. Begin by allowing children to select one pair each. Have them place the stickers on their bracelets, with the pairs close together. Invite them to choose and stick on another set, then another if one more set will fit. Join the ends of the bracelet strip together with tape, adjusting length to suit wrist size.

SNACKING:

Old fashioned animal crackers make a great snack. Pour them into a low-sided basket or bowl so the children can see and select different animals.

SINGING:

"Who Built the Ark?" "Praise the Lord, All Creation."

MORE EXPLORING:

Play Animal Charades. Have the children take turns imitating an animal's appearance or behavior for the others to guess. Explain that the game of charades is played with gestures and not sounds. Show children how to do this by acting out an animal yourself first.

THREE WISE MEN

MESSAGE:

We celebrate the birthday of Jesus.

TWIRLING:

Ask the children to stand. Choose a child to spin the globe as you lead the children in **saying: Twirl and twirl God's wonderful world! Celebrate in Children's Church!** Next, ask everyone to twirl around once, then sit down.

SHARING:

Ask: What do you like best about celebrating your birthday? *(I like cake with candles. It's fun to get presents. I like having friends to my party.)*

LISTENING:

Sing the Wise Men's Story to the familiar tune of "Three Blind Mice." Invite the children to hold up three fingers whenever they hear the number "three." **Say: In God's world, we celebrate the birthday of Jesus. Here's a song about Jesus and some birthday presents he received.**

Sing: Three Wise Men, three Wise Men,
　　　See how they go, see how they go.
　　　They followed a star that led from the West,
　　　Mile after mile without much rest.
　　　They wanted to find the child God blessed,
　　　The Three Wise Men.

　　　Three Wise Men, three Wise Men,
　　　See how they go, see how they go.
　　　In Jerusalem they asked for the promised king,
　　　For wicked King Herod, this news did sting,
　　　And his jealousy caused him to do terrible things.
　　　Beware Wise Men.

　　　Three Wise Men, three Wise Men,
　　　See where they go, see where they go.
　　　They followed that star with all their might,
　　　Until it stopped in the place just right,
　　　And Bethlehem shone with God's holy light,
　　　For Three Wise Men.

　　　Three Wise Men, three Wise Men,
　　　See where they go, see where they go.
　　　They knelt before Jesus, the newborn child,

BIBLE VERSE:

"IN THE TIME OF KING HEROD, AFTER JESUS WAS BORN IN BETHLEHEM OF JUDEA, WISE MEN FROM THE EAST CAME TO JERUSALEM."

(Matthew 2:1)

PRAY:

God of Our World, we are thankful for birthdays, especially for the birthday of your Son, Jesus. We are glad the Wise Men came to celebrate his birth. We celebrate Jesus' birthday too! Amen.

Before this king the birthday gifts they piled,
Mary and Joseph and Jesus smiled,
At the three Wise Men.

PRAYING:

Place a star sticker on the back of each child's hand. Encourage the children to look at their stars as you pray.

EXPLORING:

To create Starry Gift Bags, you will need luncheon sized paper bags, star stickers, and glitter glue pens or glitter and glue.

Explain to the children that they can use the Starry Gift Bags for future birthday celebrations. Give each child three bags as well as a sheet or partial roll of star stickers. Spread glitter pens or glitter and glue along the table. Invite the children to create beautiful starry designs. When the bags are decorated, mark the children's initials on the bottoms of the bags as you admire their creations.

SNACKING:

Since birthday cake is such a fine tradition, purchase or make birthday cake or cupcakes. Consider providing birthday plates, napkins, noisemakers, and party hats to add to the festive mood. Before serving the treat, sing the birthday song to Jesus.

SINGING:

"Jesus Loves Me"; "Children, Go Where I Send You."

MORE EXPLORING:

Play a favorite birthday game, "Pin the Tail on the Donkey." Delight the group by being the first to give it a try!

FOUR WINDS

MESSAGE:

God's world has four main directions.

TWIRLING:

Ask the children to stand. Choose a child to spin the globe as you lead the children in **saying: Twirl and twirl God's wonderful world! Celebrate in Children's Church!** Next, ask everyone to twirl around once, then sit down.

SHARING:

Ask: Can you think of some things that turn, fly, or flutter in the wind? *(Whirligigs, windmills, and pinwheels. Kites and hang gliders. Flags, windsocks, and laundry.)*

LISTENING:

Familiarize yourself with the Bible passage, Zechariah 6:1-7. Next, write the words: North, East, South, and West on four separate sheets of paper. Finally, make simple accordion fold fans for the children.

Introduce the story by asking the children to close their eyes. Explain that as you read, they are to imagine what the reading describes. Read the passage.

After the reading, have the children open their eyes as you arrange the four sheets of paper like a compass, each sheet about three feet apart. Behind each compass direction, group one fourth of the children. Hand out the paper fans. Tell the children that as you point to each group, they will use their fans to make a wind for everyone else to feel.

Reread the story. During verses 2 and 3, point first to the East, then to the North, then to the West, and then to the South, as each color of horse is mentioned. Next, at verse 6, point first to the North, then to the West, and then to the South. At the beginning of verse 7, point to the East. Conclude by **saying: In God's world, we have four main directions: North, East, South, and West**. (Point to the sheets of paper.)

PRAYING:

Invite the children to wave their fans as you pray.

BIBLE VERSE:

"The angel answered me, 'These are the four winds of heaven going out, after presenting themselves before the Lord of all the earth.'"

(Zechariah 6:5)

PRAY:

God of Our World,
we respect your gentle and your mighty winds, and the four great directions of your earth.
Amen.

EXPLORING:

To make Four Point Compasses, you will need plain paper plates, markers, paper fasteners, and construction paper as well as a ruler, pencils, hole punch, and scissors. Since paper fasteners are a choking hazard, you may not want to do this project if your children are quite young.

Prepare the paper plate compass bases by using a scissors' point to punch a small hole in each plate's center for the paper fastener to pass through. Using pencil, mark the four directions. Cut compass needles from paper, measuring and cutting strips three inches long by three quarters inches wide. You will need one needle per plate. Punch a hole at one end of each strip and cut a point at the other end.

To introduce the activity, **say: A compass is used to find directions. Today, we're going to make paper compasses.**

Bring out the paper plate compass bases and markers. Invite the children to trace over the letters of the four directions with markers. Next, give each child a compass needle and a paper fastener. Show them how to put the fastener though the compass needle, then through the plate, and finally, how to open the wings of the fastener. Encourage everyone to move the needle from point to point as you say the four directions.

SNACKING:

Further explore the number four by serving four types of snacks such as crackers, apple slices, cookies, and banana slices. Place the treats on plates in the N, E, S, W directions. Have fun calling out the directions for each treat, then invite the children to eat the treats.

SINGING:

"He's Got the Whole World"; "Lord, I Lift Your Name on High."

MORE EXPLORING:

Play a game using the four direction sheets from the story and the paper plate compasses. Let the children each have a turn moving their compass points to one of the directions and calling it out. The rest of the group will dash to that spot on the floor and shout out the name of the direction.

FIVE LOAVES

MESSAGE:

Jesus performed miracles.

TWIRLING:

Ask the children to stand. Choose a child to spin the globe as you lead the children in **saying: Twirl and twirl God's wonderful world! Celebrate in Children's Church!** Next, ask everyone to twirl around once, then sit down.

SHARING:

Ask: Can you think of a time when you were in a big crowd of people? *(At the Fourth of July fireworks. At the church Christmas play. When we went to the circus.)*

LISTENING:

Set the stage for the Feeding of the Five Thousand by locating a basket. Fill the basket with five loaves and two fish fashioned from construction paper.

Show the children the basket and begin the story.

Say: This is a story about a miracle. This is a also a story about one boy, five loaves of bread, and two fish. Jesus' followers wanted to see and hear him and be helped and healed by him. One day, Jesus crossed the Sea of Galilee and then walked up a mountainside. A crowd followed him. In this crowd was one boy with five loaves and two fish.

Jesus thought the crowd must be hungry. He talked this over with his disciples. Andrew told Jesus about the one boy with the five loaves of bread and two fish. Jesus took the basket from the one boy with the five loaves and the two fish. The disciples asked the crowd of five thousand people to sit down in the grass.

Jesus gave thanks for the five loaves and the two fish, then he handed out the food to everyone who was hungry, until all were filled. There was enough food for everyone. It was a miracle! Jesus told the disciples to gather the leftover food. They filled twelve baskets! Another miracle! The crowd saw that Jesus had turned just five loaves and two fish into a meal for thousands. They understood that Jesus could perform miracles.

BIBLE VERSE:

"THERE IS A BOY HERE WHO HAS FIVE BARLEY LOAVES AND TWO FISH. BUT WHAT ARE THEY AMONG SO MANY PEOPLE?"

(John 6:9)

105

PRAY:

God of Our World, we like to hear stories about miracles. Thank you for sending Jesus into our world! Amen.

PRAYING:

Have the children form a circle, then pass the basket around the circle. **Pray.**

EXPLORING:

Children enjoy creating with play clay. Today's challenge will be shaping five loaves of bread and two fish. This can be done as a group project or each child may make his or her own set. Purchase play clay or use the following recipe to make your own.

To make Play Clay: In a saucepan, mix two cups flour, one cup salt, and four teaspoons cream of tartar. To one cup water, add two Tablespoons of cooking oil and several drops of food coloring. Add the wet ingredients to the saucepan and stir. Cook over medium heat until the mixture begins to pull away from the sides of the pan and forms a ball. Cool, then knead. Store in an airtight container. This recipe should yield enough modeling dough for about ten children.

SNACKING:

Bread makes a perfect snack to complement this story! Since many children like white breads the best, choose a potato, cinnamon swirl, or classic white bread. Whipped butter, which spreads easily, is just right for topping the bread.

SINGING:

"Jesus Loves Me"; "I Have Decided to Follow Jesus."

MORE EXPLORING:

Play In the Basket, a memory game that calls for one basket and lots of imagination. Tell the children that the basket will be passed from person to person. Each child will pretend to add a group of five things to the basket such as five eggs, but first the player must remember what has already been added. For example, you will start the game by **saying: In the basket I am putting five loaves.** The next player will *say: In the basket are five loaves, and I am putting in five oranges.* If you have very young children or a large group, stop the memory list after the fifth person, then start the game afresh with the next player.

SIX DAYS OF CREATION

MESSAGE:
God created the world.

TWIRLING:
Ask the children to stand. Choose a child to spin the globe as you lead the children in **saying: Twirl and twirl God's wonderful world! Celebrate in Children's Church!** Next, ask everyone to twirl around once, then sit down.

SHARING:
Ask: Of all the things God created in the world, what do you like the best? *(Dolphins. Rainbows. Pretty flowers.)*

LISTENING:
Tell the story of creation, inviting the children to chime in with you as you **say: And God saw that it was good.** As a signal that this phrase is coming, give special emphasis to the word "and." Practice this a few times, then begin.

Say: In the beginning, God created the heavens and the earth. The earth was covered with oceans and darkness was everywhere. God said, "Let there be light," and there was light. AND God saw that it was good.

Then God separated the light from the darkness, calling the light "Day" and the darkness "Night." Evening came and the morning of the first day of creation.

On the second day, God created a dome to separate the waters. God called the dome "Sky" and there was water above and below the sky. AND God saw that it was good. Evening came, then morning on the second day of creation.

On the third day, God commanded the waters under the sky to come together so there would be dry ground. God called the dry ground "Earth," and he called the waters that were gathered together "Seas." God commanded that the earth put forth vegetables and fruitful trees of every kind. AND God saw that it was good. Evening came, then morning of the third day of creation.

On the fourth day, God created two great lights in the sky. The greater light was for the day and the lesser light was for the night. AND God saw that it was good. Evening came, then morning on the fourth day of creation.

BIBLE VERSE:
"God saw everything that he had made, and indeed, it was very good. And there was evening and there was morning, the sixth day."

(Genesis 1:31)

PRAY:

God of Our
World,
we love your
wonderful
creation: the day
and the night,
the sky and the
ocean,
the land and the
plants,
the sun and the
moon,
the sea
creatures and
birds,
and the animals
and the people.
Amen.

NUMBERS

108

On the fifth day, God commanded the seas to be filled with many sea creatures. God also created all the birds of the air. AND God saw that it was good. Evening came, then morning on the fifth day of creation.

On the sixth day of creation, God ordered that the earth be filled with every kind of farm animal and wild animal, reptiles and many creeping things. AND God saw that it was good. Then God created man and woman and blessed them. Evening came, then morning on the sixth day of creation. AND God saw that it was good.

PRAYING:

Have the children form a circle, then pass a globe around the circle. **Say: This is the world God created. Place the globe in the center of the circle. Invite the children to look at it as you say the prayer.**

EXPLORING:

Play Twirl-A-Whirl to celebrate God's creation. Before Children's Church, draw simple pictures that symbolize day, night, sky, ocean, land, plants, animals, and people.

When it's time for the game, place the pictures in a wide circle like the hours on a clock. Have the children stand in a circle around the circle of pictures.

To play, choose a child to step into the center of the circle, and twirl around several times, with one arm outstretched. When the child stops twirling, ask the child to say the name of the part of creation his or her arm is pointing toward (sun, plants, animals.) When the child responds, the group is to shout, "It is good!" Let every child have at least one turn.

SNACKING:

Invite the children to celebrate the fourth day of creation by creating their own Sun Crackers and Moon Crackers. Purchase round crackers and squirt cheese. Have children use the cheese to draw a smiling face or sun rays on the Sun Crackers and a crescent or crater dots on the Moon Crackers.

SINGING:

"He's Got the Whole World"; "O God in Heaven (Verse 1)."

MORE EXPLORING:

Give your young artists an opportunity to illustrate their favorite parts of creation. Provide them with crayons, markers, or watercolors. Talk to the children about what they are illustrating as they work. Consider labeling and displaying their pictures for the congregation to enjoy.

REST ON THE SEVENTH DAY

MESSAGE:

We come to church on the sabbath.

TWIRLING:

Ask the children to stand. Choose a child to spin the globe as you lead the children in **saying: Twirl and twirl God's wonderful world! Celebrate in Children's Church!** Next, ask everyone to twirl around once, then sit down.

SHARING:

Ask: What is something you like about coming to church? *(I like hearing stories and playing games. It's fun to see my friends. I like to hear the loud organ.)*

LISTENING:

Lead the children through this action story that describes a Sunday morning. Demonstrate a simple action for each activity.

Say: On the seventh day of creation, God rested. In time, this became, the sabbath, a day of worship. We go to church on our sabbath, which is Sunday. Let's act out a Sunday morning.

Wake up! Open your eyes! Yawn and stretch. Jump out of bed. (Have everyone stand up.) **Run to the breakfast table.** (Have everyone sit down.) **Sip your juice. Crunch your toast. Spoon up your scrambled egg. Say "thanks" to Mom or Dad.** (Have everyone stand up.) **Brush your teeth. Put on your church clothes. Wave goodbye to your cat.**

You're there! Take a seat in Sunday school. (Have everyone take a seat.) **Sunday school is over!** (Have everyone stand up.) **Time for worship. Shake hands with the greeter. Say "good morning" to the usher. Sit in your pew.** (Have everyone sit down.) **Look up at the tall windows and the cross. Look around at all the families. Smile when you hear the bells ring. Wiggle in your seat as the pastor and the choir come in. Hum along with the choir's song. Listen to the pastor.**

Stand and walk with your Children's Church teacher. (Have everyone stand up.) **Play a twirling game.** (Have everyone sit down.) **Laugh with your friends. Clap during the story. Bow your head when you pray. Eat a fun snack. Color a pretty picture. Show the picture to your mom or dad.** (Have everyone stand up.) **It's time to go!**

BIBLE VERSE:

"I WAS GLAD WHEN THEY SAID TO ME, 'LET US TO GO THE HOUSE OF THE LORD!'" (Psalm 122:1)

PRAY:

God of Our
World,
we're glad that
on Sunday,
we come to your
house.
Amen.

PRAYING:

Lead the children in the old favorite: Here is the church, here is the steeple, open the doors to see all the people. Ask them to keep their hands folded as a church for the prayer.

EXPLORING:

To create a Happy Place, Happy Face Banner, you will need plain paper plates, crayons, a roll of crepe paper streamer or adding machine tape, and a stapler. Give the children the plates and crayons, inviting them each to draw a happy face on one or more plates. **Say: We're making happy faces because our church is a happy place to come on Sundays and other days, too.**

When the faces are finished, staple them side by side along the roll of paper. Print the phrases, "Happy Place" and "Happy Faces" on two paper plates, putting them at each end of the banner. Hang the banner somewhere near the entrance to your church.

SNACKING:

Happy Face Cookies will make everyone smile! Buy several tubes of frosting, as well as sugar cookies. Invite each child to take a turn drawing a happy face with frosting. Admire all the cookie faces, before the children enjoy them for a snack. Go on to round two of cookie decorating if you like.

SINGING:

"Happy All the Time"; "O God in Heaven (Verse 1)."

MORE EXPLORING:

Sing "If You're Happy And You Know It" with the following lines. Lead the song, asking the children to join in:

If you're happy and you know it, go to church!
If you're happy and you know it, go to church!
If you're happy and you know it,
Then your face will surely show it.
If you're happy and you know it, go to church!

Add these lines to continue the song:
If you're happy and you know it, sing a hymn.
   "   " shake a hand.
   "   " pray with friends.
   "   " read the Bible.
   "   " share a snack.
   "   " bring a friend.

HOLiDAYS in God's World

STARS FOR EPIPHANY

MESSAGE:

The wise men followed a star to find Jesus.

TWIRLING:

Ask the children to stand. Choose a child to spin the globe as you lead the children in **saying: Twirl and twirl God's wonderful world! Celebrate in Children's Church!** Next, ask everyone to twirl around once, then sit down.

SHARING:

Ask: Can you tell us a Christmas present that you or your family gave to someone this Christmas? *(We gave my Grandpa a golf club. We made cookies for all of our neighbors.)*

LISTENING:

Tell the children that today's story is about a star. Every time they hear the word "star" or "stars," they are to pretend to point to a bright star in the sky. Practice this a few times, then begin.

Say: After Jesus was born, wise men from the east noticed a star (pause) **shining brightly in the night sky. They began to follow the star.** (pause) **They followed the star,** (pause) **and followed the star,** (pause) **and followed the star** (pause) **until the star** (pause) **stopped over the place where the child Jesus was. When the wise men who were following the star** (pause) **saw that the star** (pause) **had stopped there, they were overwhelmed with joy.**

BIBLE VERSE:

"when they saw that the star had stopped, they were overwhelmed with joy."

(Matthew 2:10)

111

PRAY:

God of Our World, we're glad the wise men came from afar and followed that beautiful, important star. Amen.

They went into the house and found the mother, Mary, with her child, Jesus. They knelt down and honored him. The wise men gave him presents of gold and frankincense and myrrh. What a beautiful star (pause) that must have been to guide the wise men to Jesus. Today, we celebrate that star (pause) at Epiphany. Epiphany comes just a short time after Christmas. Epiphany is the celebration of the wise men's visit and the coming of Jesus, our Savior, into the world. Hooray for that important star! (pause)

PRAYING:

Have the children point to a pretend star one more time. **Pray.**

EXPLORING:

Send the children on a Star Scavenger Hunt. Before Children's Church, cut six or seven sheets of paper into the shape of a star or decorate sheets of paper with stars. On each starry sheet, write a clue that will send children from one location to another. For example: "This is where we hang our coats." (The clue is on the coat rack.) "This is where we put our trash." (The clue is on the trash can.) Or "This is where we keep our Bibles." (The clue is on the bookcase.) The next clue should be easy to spot once the children get to that location but not visible from far away. You may need to secure the clues with tape.

At the end of the Star Scavenger Hunt, the children will find a package with tiny gifts and a snack inside. Dollar stores and party stores are good places to find inexpensive trinkets. The snack can simply be a favorite brand of cookies. Put the trinkets and snack into a box, wrap the box in colorful paper, and tie with a ribbon. Add a gift tag if you like.

To begin, explain to the children that they are going on a Star Scavenger Hunt in honor of the wise men. Start the hunt by saying a clue that will send the children to the first location. If you have readers, ask them to take turns reading the clue to the group once a clue is found. If you don't have readers, read the clues yourself.

SNACKING:

Invite the children to take turns unwrapping the present they found at the end of the Star Scavenger Hunt. Explain that the custom of giving presents at Christmas time is linked to the wise men who brought gifts to Jesus. Let the children help hand out the trinkets and serve the snack.

SINGING:

"Father, We Thank Thee"; "The Wise May Bring Their Learning."

HOLIDAYS

MORE EXPLORING:

To make Glittery Stars, you will need a foam sheet (available in craft departments) or cardboard, duct tape or another strong tape, glue, glitter, construction paper, a dish, and several shallow pans or cookie sheets.

Before Children's Church, cut a star shape from a foam sheet or cardboard. If you have a star shaped cookie cutter, use that as a stencil. (One easy way to create a star shaped stencil is to overlap equilateral triangles cut from paper. Tape them together with one point of one triangle facing upward and one point of another triangle facing downward.) Once you have cut out a star shape from a foam sheet or cardboard, put a loop of duct tape on the back to form a handle.

Explain to the children that they are going to create Glittery Stars. Pour glue into the bottom of the dish. Give each child a piece of construction paper. Dip the star shape into the glue and press it onto the construction paper in two or three places, adding more glue each time. Invite the children to pour glitter over the glue, shaking the excess into the pans. When the glue is dry, hang the Glittery Stars in celebration of Epiphany.

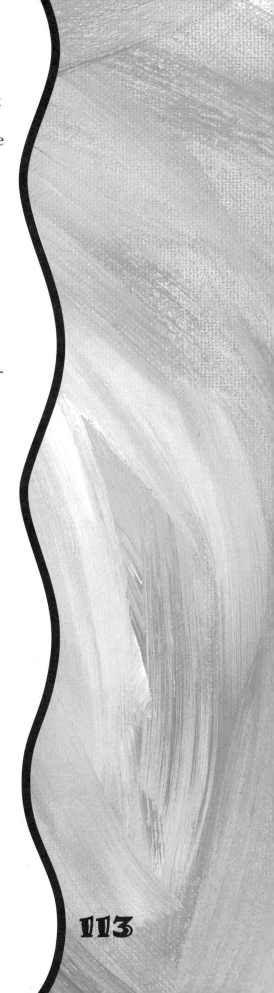

BIBLE VERSE:

"THIS IS MY COMMANDMENT, THAT YOU LOVE ONE ANOTHER AS I HAVE LOVED YOU."

(John 15:12)

HOLIDAYS

HEARTS FOR VALENTINE'S DAY

MESSAGE:

God wants us to love others.

TWIRLING:

Ask the children to stand. Choose a child to spin the globe as you lead the children in **saying: Twirl and twirl God's wonderful world! Celebrate in Children's Church!** Next, ask everyone to twirl around once, then sit down.

SHARING:

Ask: Can you tell us the name of someone you love? *(I love Liza. I love my Uncle Harrison. I love my mom and my dad and my cat.)*

LISTENING:

As you tell part of the story, you will slowly cut out a paper heart. Although standard size paper is fine, consider using a large sheet of wrapping paper to make a giant heart. Folding a sheet of paper in half, then cutting one side of the heart, will create a symmetrical heart. If you haven't used this technique for cutting out a paper heart, practice this on scrap paper.

Say: Jesus taught us many lessons, but one of his most important lessons is that God wants us to love one another. Read the Bible verse. **Jesus wants us to love one another every single day, but Valentine's Day is a holiday when we think especially about loving one another.**

Bring out the folded paper. Very slowly begin to cut out a heart. **Say: I love** (as you cut, say the name of each child.) **And while I've been naming all of you, my wonderful Children's Church kids, I've cut out a shape. A Valentine's Day shape. Ask: Does anyone know what that shape is?** (After the children *call out: a heart,* open the heart and hold it up.) **That's right! A Valentine's Day heart to show my love for each of you!**

PRAYING:

Hold up the paper heart and ask the children to look at it as you pray.

EXPLORING:

For Paper Valentines, gather a variety of traditional paper goods used in making valentines: doilies; red, pink, and white construction paper; a package of inexpensive children's valentines; and stickers. You will also need glue, scissors, and markers. Encourage the children to make several valentines each.

Suggest that the children give out their valentines right after church. Along with one for their parents, encourage them to give valentines to the pastor, a bigger kid, teenager, or an adult friend, a visitor, or an elderly member of your congregation.

SNACKING:

Now invite the children to decorate edible valentines! Bake or purchase cupcakes or iced cookies. Offer red, pink, and white sprinkles and candy hearts for the children to put on top.

SINGING:

"Down in My Heart"; "O, How He Loves You and Me."

MORE EXPLORING:

Play the I Love Game using the paper valentine you cut during the story. Have the children form a circle. Tell them that you will call out a category, then send the paper valentine around the circle. When it's their turn to hold the valentine, they are to name someone they love who fits that category. Categories might include: Relatives, School Friends, Church Members, Neighbors, and Far Away Friends.

PRAY:

God of Our World,
paper hearts remind us of love! Thank you for loving us and for the love of Jesus. Help us to love one another each and every day. Amen.

BIBLE VERSE:

"THEN THOSE WHO WENT AHEAD AND THOSE WHO FOLLOWED WERE SHOUTING, 'HOSANNA! BLESSED IS THE ONE WHO COMES IN THE NAME OF THE LORD!'"

(Mark 11:9)

THREE CHEERS PALM SUNDAY

MESSAGE:

Jesus is our Savior.

SHARING:

Ask: Have you ever cheered for someone or something? *(I cheer for my favorite basketball team. I cheered at field day at school. My sister and I cheered when my mom said we were going to Disneyland.)*

LISTENING:

Play the part of the donkey as you tell the story of Jesus' entry into Jerusalem. Consider cutting out a pair of donkey ears from construction paper and fastening them to a paper ring that fits around your head.

Say: Hee-haw, he-haw. I'm Dina the Donkey, and I'm the one who gave Jesus a ride into Jerusalem before Passover. I live outside the city, but I do go to the big city to do errands with my owner. On that day, I was quietly munching hay, when a very interesting man and his followers came near. His followers led me over to the man, who spoke softly to me and patted my nose. I liked him right away. You know, we donkeys can be stubborn and mean if we want to, but I decided I wanted to be nice to this man.

The man got on my back, and we began to walk toward the city. One of his followers called him "Jesus." As we went along the road, people came out from their houses to walk with us. Workers left the fields too and shoppers on their way to market joined us. Everyone was happy and excited to see Jesus. They talked about the wonderful things he had said and done. They all agreed that Jesus was their savior and king.

Soon there was a crowd as far as you could see. The people began cheering for Jesus as they took off their cloaks and cut palm branches to lay in the road. My hoofs clopped over the most beautiful and the most ragged coats, because there were very rich and very poor people in the crowd. Jesus sat calmly on my back, and as the crowds began to press in closer and closer to see and touch him, he spoke gentle words to me; and I was not afraid of all those people.

Finally, he slid from my back and gave me to a kind person who served me water and a bit of food before taking me

HOLIDAYS

116

home. That was the most amazing day because I carried Jesus, the Savior, into Jerusalem. Hee-haw! That's the end of my story.

PRAYING:

Have the children bow their heads for the prayer.

EXPLORING:

In the spirit of Palm Sunday, lead cheers for Jesus! Consider making crepe paper pom poms for the children to wave. For each pom pom, wrap crepe paper streamers six or seven times around the width of a Bible or other book. Slip a twist tie or piece of yarn along the binding side of the Bible to gather the crepe paper together, then twist the twist tie or knot the yarn. Cut the crepe paper along the pages' side to finish the pom pom. Fluff by giving the pom pom several good shakes.

Lead the children in these cheers:

Jesus, Jesus is the one!
He is God's only son!
Jesus, Jesus is the one!
Yeah, Jesus!
H-O-S-A-N-N-A!
Hosanna is what we say!
Hosanna, hosanna, hosanna!
One-two-three-four!
Who are we cheering for?
Jesus! Jesus! Jesus!
Zip Boom Ba!
Ra Ra Ra!
Hooray for Jesus!
Hooray for Jesus!
Hooray for Jesus!
Ra Ra Ra!
Zip Boom Ba!

SNACKING:

When we think of parades and cheering crowds, we think of a snack that is served by venders such as popcorn, hot pretzels, slushy drinks, or ice cream sandwiches. Choose something for your children to enjoy.

MORE EXPLORING:

Let each child lead the others around the room in a Palm Parade, using the palms of their hands. Explain that the palm tree got its name because its fronds look like the palms of people's hands. Have the leader make hand and palm motions for everyone to follow.

PRAY:

God of Our World, thank you for Bible stories and thank you for our Savior, Jesus Christ. Amen.

117

BiBLe VeRSe:

"He is not here; for he has Been Raised, as He said. Come, See the place where He Lay."

(Matthew 28:6)

HOLiDaYS

NEW LIFE AT EASTER

MESSAGE:

God gave Jesus new life after his death.

SHARING:

Ask: In God's world of plants and animals, have you seen any signs of new life this spring? *(I saw baby chicks. There are dandelions growing in my yard. Trees are getting new leaves.)*

LISTENING:

Invite the children to join in the story by *saying: New Life!* every time you point to them.

Say: After Jesus died, he was laid into a small room cut into a rock wall. This room was called a "tomb." A large rock was rolled over the opening of the tomb, just like a door. Jesus' tomb was in a garden.

Springtime had come to the garden. Signs of the seasons were everywhere. Baby birds were hatching in their nests. (Point: "new life.") **Bright green leaves were starting to grow on tree branches.** (Point: "new life.") **Baby rabbits hopped behind their mother.** (Point: "new life.") **Flower blossoms of yellow, pink, and orange opened under the warm sun.** (Point: "new life.") **Seeds pushed up through the ground.** (Point: "new life.") **Honeybees hatched and flew outside the beehive for the first time.** (Point: "new life.") **And tadpoles swam in the water trough.** (Point: "new life.")

Night fell and the garden was dark, until an angel came shining bright as lightning. The angel rolled away the stone, and God gave Jesus new life. (Point: "new life.") **Jesus stood and walked out of the tomb and into the garden full of** (Point: "new life.") **light.**

As the sun came up, the people who loved Jesus went to the garden to visit his grave. They were surprised to see that the stone was rolled away from the tomb and even more amazed when the angel told them that Jesus was raised from the dead. As the people turned to leave, they met Jesus! God had given him (Point: "new life.")**new life!**

PRAYING:

Have the children hold their arms over their heads in the shape of an egg. **Say: Eggs and chicks have been a symbol of new life for many years. Pray.**

EXPLORING:

Play three games with eggs! You'll need one plastic egg and one spoon for each child, and a chick sticker to put inside each egg. Before Children's Church, cut apart the chick stickers, if necessary; and put one inside each egg. Hide the eggs around the room or in an area nearby.

Say: Since eggs and chicks are a symbol of new life, let's play some games using eggs that children have played for hundreds of years.

Lead the children in the following three games:

Egg Hunt: Invite the children to find one plastic egg each. When they discover the sticker, ask them to keep the chick inside the egg until after the game.

Egg Balance: Have children form a circle. Give each child a spoon and an egg. Have her or him try to carry the egg on the spoon as she or he walks in a circle.

Egg Roll: Have the children place their eggs on the floor in front of them. Tell them to use their spoons to roll their plastic eggs to the other side of the room or around the room.

When the games are finished, children may put the stickers on their eggs.

SNACK:

Find signs of new life on the candy aisle in the form of marshmallow chicks and/or or use a chick cookie cutter to cut chick shapes from slices of potato bread, which has a yellow hue.

SINGING:

"Praise the Lord Together"; "Hosanna in the Highest."

MORE EXPLORING:

Children will have fun following your lead as you imitate sounds of new life; a human baby (waa, waa); a chick (cheep, cheep); a duckling (quack, quack); a lamb (baa, baa); a donkey colt (hee-haw); a puppy (yip, yip); a kitten (mew, mew); a piglet (oink, oink); and a goat kid (naa, naa).

Try a truly imaginary venture by asking children to create the pretend sounds of new seeds coming up, flowers blooming, tree leaves unfolding, grass growing, and vines curling.

PRAY:

God of Our World,
we believe in new life,
which we see all around us,
and we believe you gave Jesus new life after his death.
Amen.

BIBLE VERSE:

"We give thanks to you, O God; we give thanks; your name is near. People tell of your wondrous deeds."

(Psalm 75:1)

CORNUCOPIAS OF THANKS

MESSAGE:

We give thanks to God.

TWIRLING:

Ask the children to stand. Choose a child to spin the globe as you lead the children in **saying: Twirl and twirl God's wonderful world! Celebrate in Children's Church!** Next, ask everyone to twirl around once, then sit down.

SHARING:

Ask: What is something you like about Thanksgiving? *(I like going to my Grandma's. I like to watch the parade. The dinner is so delicious.)*

LISTENING:

Explain to the children that they will help you tell the story. Each time you name a category, they will take a turn adding something in that category for which they are thankful.

Say: Once upon a time, there was a wonderful group of kids who went to Children's Church at (Have the children say the name of the church.) **They were thankful to God for all of the blessings in their lives. One Sunday near Thanksgiving, their teacher read this Bible verse.** (Read the verse.) **Their teacher explained that "thanksgiving" means "to give thanks to God." Then the teacher said, "Let's play the Thanksgiving Game. I'll name a category. Then each of you will name something in that category that you are thankful for."**

The first category called out was "Foods." Then all of the kids named a food they were thankful for. (Have the children each name a food.)

The next category called out was "People." Then all of the kids named a person they were thankful for. (Have the children each name a person.)

The next category called out was "Toys." Then all of the kids named a toy they were thankful for. (Have the children each name a toy they are thankful for.)

The next category called out was "Places." Then all of the kids named a place they were thankful for. (Have the children each name a place they are thankful for.)

The last category called out was "Anything at All." The kids named lots of interesting things they were thankful for. (Have the children name anything at all they are thankful for.) **What a wonderful group of kids came to Children's Church that day. Their teacher was very thankful to know each and every one of them! The End.**

PRAYING:

Have the children form a circle. Ask them to *say: Thanks, God.*

EXPLORING:

To make Paper Bag Cornucopias, you will need brown luncheon bags, women's or cooking magazines, scissors, and a stapler or glue. Before Children's Church, make a sample cornucopia to show the children. Roll over the top of a paper bag an inch or two. Then twist the bottom of the bag into the curved shape of a cornucopia. The children will staple or glue two or three magazine pictures of food inside the cornucopia. You may look through the magazines ahead of time, tear out, and trim the pictures or have the children do this themselves. Staple or glue two or three food pictures inside your sample cornucopia.

Say: Today, in honor of Thanksgiving, we're going to make cornucopias. Cornucopia means "horn of plenty." We see cornucopias at Thanksgiving time, especially on greeting cards and paper plates and napkins. Cornucopias are usually filled with fruits and vegetables. They represent God's plentiful blessings.

Show the children the sample cornucopia, then help them fold and twist their bags into their own cornucopias. Next, have them each staple or glue two or three food pictures inside. Suggest that they use their cornucopias to decorate their kitchens or dinner tables over the Thanksgiving holiday.

SNACK:

Fill one or several paper cornucopias with washed fruit. Set out the cornucopias, then invite the children to each choose a piece of fruit.

SINGING:

"Praise Him, Praise Him"; "For Health and Strength."

MORE EXPLORING:

Invite the children to color pictures of something for which they are thankful. Have them sign their names to the pictures. Write a brief note to go along with the pictures and package them up to mail to one or several members of your church who could use a bit of extra attention.

PRAY:

God of Our World, thanks for everything! Amen.

"AND SUDDENLY THERE WAS WITH THE ANGEL A MULTITUDE OF THE HEAVENLY HOST, PRAISING GOD."

(Luke 2:13)

HOLIDAYS

CHRISTMAS ANGELS

MESSAGE:

We sing of Christmas angels.

SHARING:

Ask: Do you have any Christmas decorations at your house that have angels on them? (*We have lots of angel ornaments. There is an angel at the top of our tree. My aunt made me an angel pillow.*)

LISTENING:

For the story, bring an angel ornament, figurine, or illustration. Begin by showing this to the children, and passing it around, if practical.

Say: Angels play an important role in the Christmas story because they bring the good news that Jesus, the Savior, was coming into the world. First the angel, Gabriel, appeared to Mary. Gabriel told Mary that she was truly blessed by God and that God was with her. Mary was confused about what he meant, so Gabriel told her not to be afraid. He explained that God was pleased with her and would create in her a baby. The baby would be a special baby boy, who would be God's only son. Mary wondered how this would happen. The angel told her that nothing was impossible with God.

Then an angel appeared to Joseph in a dream telling him not to be worried or afraid. The angel explained that Mary's baby came from the Holy Spirit of God and that the baby would be a boy. He told Joseph that the baby should be named "Jesus" because he would save the people.

On the night when Jesus was born, an angel appeared to announce the happy news to shepherds keeping watch over their flock of sheep in a field. The angel told the shepherds to go find the baby who was lying in a manger in Bethlehem. Then suddenly a whole group of angels joined the other angel. The angels sang praises to God.

An angel appeared to Mary, to Joseph, and to the shepherds. When we sing songs about Christmas and the birth of Jesus, we often sing about angels.

PRAYING:

Have the children form halos above their heads with their hands. **Pray**.

EXPLORING:

It's time to lead the children in singing about those Christmas angels! You'll need Christmas tapes or CDs and a player or a singer or musician to lead the singing.

Angels appear in the following: "While Shepherds Watched Their Flocks," "The First Noel," "It Came Upon the Midnight Clear," "Hark! The Herald Angels Sing," "Silent Night," "Go Tell It on the Mountain," "Angels We Have Heard on High," "Angels From the Realms of Glory," "The Snow Lay on the Ground," and others. As they sing, ask the children to listen carefully for the words "angel" or "angels."

SNACKING:

Serve Marshmallow Angels! You'll need marshmallow creme, mini-marshmallows, and white bread slices, as well as knives and plates. This snack may be made ahead of time, or, depending on the skill level of your children, may be assembled by them.

To create a Marshmallow Angel, place a slice of bread on a plate and spread with marshmallow creme. With a knife, cut the bread in half diagonally to form two triangles. Cut one of these triangles in half to make two smaller triangles. Arrange the larger triangle as the angel body and the two smaller triangles as the angel wings. Use a mini-marshmallow to be the angel's head.

SINGING:

"This Little Light of Mine"; "Long, Long Ago."

MORE EXPLORING:

Let your group pretend to be Christmas angels. If your church has a costume collection, allow the children to wear the wings and halos. If not, purchase tinsel garland for halos. Cut the garland into fifteen-inch lengths, one per child, and make a loop, securing with tape.

The angels can fly about to the strains of Christmas carols; pretend to visit Mary, Joseph, and the shepherds; and freeze into angelic poses.

PRAY:

God of Our World, thank you for the Christmas angels who told of the coming of Jesus. Amen.

123

"SO THeY
WeNT
WiTH
HASTe AND
FOUND
MARY AND
JOSePH,
AND THe
CHiLD
LYiNG iN
THe
MANGeR."

(Luke 2:16)

CHRISTMAS SHEPHERDS

MeSSAGe:

We visit one another.

SHARiNG:

Ask: Do you remember a time when you visited someone or someone visited you? *(We visit my grandma and grandpa. My cousins came over yesterday. I go to visit my dad on weekends.)*

LiSTeNiNG:

Prepare for the storytelling by making a simple shepherd's headdress for yourself. A piece of cloth or towel secured with a sash or scarf will work well.

Say: Hello! I'm a shepherd. My parents are shepherds and their parents were shepherds and my great-grandparents and my great-great-grandparents were shepherds, too. We've all been shepherds all the way back to Bible times. I want to read to you a story from the Bible about the first people to visit Baby Jesus and guess what? They were shepherds!

Read Luke 2:8-20.

Say: As a shepherd, I'm very proud to read you a story about some very important shepherds who visited a very important baby long ago on a very important night! What a very important visit that was!

PRAYiNG:

Have the children bow their heads for the prayer.

eXPLORiNG:

To make Welcome Bags, you will need paper lunch bags, decorations such as recycled Christmas cards and/or Christmas stickers, scissors, glue, tape, and crayons. You will also need some welcome gifts to go inside the bags such as candy canes, wrapped gingerbread people, stickers, holidays pencils, or other inexpensive items.

Invite the children to decorate a bag, explaining that they are to give their bags to someone they visit, someone who visits them, or to a family visiting the church. When the bags are ready, allow the children to put one of each type of welcome gifts into their bags. Fold the top of the bags over and have the children secure them with a sticker or tape.

SNACKING:

'Tis the season to taste a variety of Christmas cookies. Try to find or make several types for the children to taste such as gingerbread, shortbread, chocolate chip, sugar, oatmeal, or cocoa. Serve with milk or juice.

SINGING:

"This Little Light of Mine"; "Long, Long Ago."

MORE EXPLORING:

Play the Shepherds Circle Game. Have the children stand in a circle. Explain that one by one everyone will join hands (or link elbows) in the walk to visit Baby Jesus. You will start by choosing a shepherd to slip out of the circle and hold hands (or link elbows) with you. You two will walk completely around the circle *repeating: The shepherds walk to visit Jesus.* Once around the circle, choose another shepherd to join you two in walking around the circle. Continue choosing shepherds until the circle is empty. Have the line of shepherds form a new circle and stop in place. Ask all the shepherds to *repeat after you: Welcome to the world, Baby Jesus!* Go another round or two, as time permits.

PRAY:

God of Our World, we are glad that shepherds visited Baby Jesus, and we are glad to visit with others too, especially at Christmas. Amen.

Notes

126

Notes

Notes